CERC
Christian Educational
W9-BON-435
Roseville, MN 55113

HABITS of the HEART

SELF-DISCIPLINE FOR THE NOT-SO-DISCIPLINED

KATHY BABBITT

Wolgemuth & Hyatt, Publishers, Inc.
Brentwood, Tennessee

The mission of Wolgemuth & Hyatt, Publishers, Inc. is to publish and distribute books that lead individuals toward:

- A personal faith in the one true God: Father, Son, and Holy Spirit;
- A lifestyle of practical discipleship; and
- A worldview that is consistent with the historic, Christian faith.

Moreover, the company endeavors to accomplish this mission at a reasonable profit and in a manner which glorifies God and serves His Kingdom.

© 1990 by Kathy J. Babbitt
All rights reserved. Published September 1990. First edition.

No part of this publication may be reproduced, stored in a retrieval system, or transmitted in any form by any means, electronic, mechanical, photocopy, recording, or otherwise, without the prior written permission of the publisher, except for brief quotations in critical reviews or articles.

Unless otherwise noted, all scripture quotations are from the Holy Bible, New International Version. © 1973, 1978, 1984 International Bible Society. Used by permission of Zondervan Bible Publishers.

Wolgemuth & Hyatt, Publishers, Inc.
1749 Mallory Lane, Suite 110, Brentwood, Tennessee 37027.

Printed in the United States of America.

97 96 95 94 93 92 91 90   8 7 6 5 4 3 2 1

Library of Congress Cataloging-in-Publication Data

Babbitt, Kathy J.
     Habits of the heart : self-discipline for the not-so-disciplined /
Kathy Babbitt. — 1st ed.
          p.   cm.
     Includes bibliographical references.
     ISBN 1-56121-018-8
     1. Self-control — Religious aspects — Christianity.   I. Title.
BV4647.S39B32   1990
241'.4 — dc20   90-38106
                                                                      CIP

To Dave,
who has become my beloved.

CONTENTS

ACKNOWLEDGMENTS

With heartfelt appreciation, my thanks go to Max and Margie Anders for their willingness to offer assistance in this project. Their depth of knowledge and attention to detail, both theological and grammatical, helped to fine-tune the manuscript.

I am also deeply grateful for R. Eileen Thacker and the joy with which she reviewed the manuscript. Her creative insights and enthusiasm for both the content and the craft added a satisfying dimension in its preparation.

It was a gratifying experience to obtain Julie's story (chapter 11). With Julie's permission, her's is the only name that has not been changed. It is her desire that many be encouraged through the trials she has endured.

And, then to my husband, Dave, who has had the courage to follow his dreams, with the faith in God, patience, and discipline to see them become reality. And, finally, for encouraging and supporting me to follow mine as well.

AUTHOR'S NOTE

This is not meant to be a theological, psychological, or medical work. Should questions arise in these areas, please consult with a professional in the respective field.

All the names except one in the illustrations have been changed. Stories are a compilation of personal experience, case histories of people I have known, a combination of several identities, or in some cases created to fit the need.

FOREWORD

In order to be free to sail the seven seas, we must make ourselves a slave to the compass. Each of us is a slave to something. We are either a slave to self-discipline, or we are a slave to circumstances. We don't like it, but that's the way it is.

We can either be a slave to the toothbrush and free from cavities, or we can be free from the toothbrush and a slave to cavities. We cannot be free from both. That kind of freedom, total freedom, doesn't exist.

One of the most important things in life, then, is for us to choose well what we are going to be a slave to. It determines the outcome of our life. That's where self-discipline comes in.

This is a book on self-discipline, and like all good books, it is a product not of distant speculation, but of real life. Failure has been the back door to success for Kathy. The introduction alone is sufficient for her to earn a hearing on this subject. Anyone who has gone through what Kathy has gone through, and can not only function normally, but thrive, has my attention.

Helpful hints, keen insights, and gentle persuasion rise from the pages like helium balloons at the opening ceremonies of the Olympic games. There is a constant stream of practical ways to get control of life an inch at a time.

Sometimes the hints are so self-evident, you want to smack your forehead and say, "Why didn't I think of that?" The unpretentious stories make it easy reading. As Kathy tells you about her friends you will see yourself in many of the stories. As she talks about Bruce or Louise or Holly, she could just as easily be using your name.

Some of the chapters may make you uncomfortable. They did me. They were the ones I needed the most.

I found myself wanting to be more disciplined as a result of reading this book. In fact, I am more disciplined as a result of reading this book. I guess that is the best recommendation I could give it. I think you'll find the same happening with you.

Max Anders
Author of *30 Days to Understanding the Bible*

INTRODUCTION

Y ou fool!" declared the young lady's husband. He had just learned
that his wife had asked the Lord four years earlier to teach her
all she needed to know in order to write a book on self-discipline.
Having an interest in the subject and finding a void on the market,
she had innocently offered her request to the Lord.

Now, however, she wondered if the nightmare she had brought
on her family was worth the answered prayer. Mononucleosis on
top of a serious case of malaria had thrown her immune system into
chaos. She was plagued with chemical and food allergies which literally drove her out of her mind. Allergies cause many people to experience bloating in their stomachs or other body tissues. For her,
the swelling occurred in her brain, resulting in violent flare-ups
coupled with erratic behavior.

Others have suffered for years and spent thousands of dollars
trying to find relief. In her case the problem was isolated in a matter of weeks to eggs, milk, wheat, and certain fruits, vegetables,
spices, and meats—all of which could no longer be a part of her
diet. The few foods left, most of them exotic, could be eaten only
every four days so that further allergies would not develop. One
day she would make mayonnaise out of goose eggs and walnut oil.
Another day it would be made out of duck eggs and sesame oil. She
lived for her potato day. It was the only day in four that she was
really full.

To make matters worse, she had to eat every half-hour to maintain her blood sugar level, or she would pass out. But one bite of an offending food could make her a basket case for three days—until the food had time to work its way out of her system. Because she was so severely limited in what she could eat, she knew that her very survival depended upon self-discipline.

After about eight months of this maddening eating schedule, she was starting to react to everything. No longer could she eat rice cakes or garbanzo muffins. She was becoming a permanent mental case.

Then one morning she remembered that her supplier of distilled water said the distiller wasn't working right. So the young lady immediately bought a gallon of distilled water. By the end of the day she was almost sane again. And by the next day she felt as normal as she had in months. They checked the distiller and discovered that the hoses were attached backwards. She had been drinking months of residue that had built up in the distiller!

About a week later, while her husband was in Chicago for training, she realized that she was literally starving herself to death on the diet. Her motivation was always fear—fear that she would eat something on the wrong day and build up even more allergies; fear that she couldn't control her actions if she ate an impure food. One day she ate meat from the health food store and went on a rampage. Later, the paprika in the meat was singled out as the menace. The doctors urged her to go to an environmentally-controlled clinic, similar to living in a bubble, for one month at a cost of thirteen thousand dollars. She was almost to the end of her endurance.

I was that young lady. And the Lord did teach me much about self-discipline. And He did enable me to write a book about the subject. You are reading the result of that effort. But let me tell you how this scenario ended.

I hadn't wanted to ask God to heal me because I wasn't sure if I had learned everything He wanted me to through this experience. I was convinced that one day—maybe five years down the road—the allergy problem would be behind me. But one evening, after the children were in bed and Dave was many thousands of miles away in Chicago, I felt that now was the time to ask God for complete and total healing of the physical ills that were plaguing not only me, but our family as well.

So I asked God to touch my body. I believed He did. Yet there was the test. I went to the kitchen and made a piece of toast that contained all the ingredients I was allergic to and spread it with margarine I didn't dare eat. I took this simple piece of toast up to my bedroom, sat on the bed, and offered it as a sacrifice to the Lord.

But there was that underlying fear. If I took one bite and the Lord hadn't chosen to heal me right then, I was taking a very grave risk. Dave was in Chicago, and I was responsible for the kids for the next week. One bite would turn me into an incompetent, vicious, mentally ill mother for three days.

I read more Scripture and prayed until I was convinced that this was the step God wanted me to take. And then I continued to struggle. I was amazed at how hard it was to take that first bite. Finally, by faith, I ate the piece of toast. I had no immediate reaction.

The next morning I told the girls what I had done and that I would be eating breakfast with them. They just sat there with their mouths hanging open. They knew all too well the consequences of eating an allergy food, and they were frightened. All day long I continued to eat foods to which I was allergic. I used hairspray I normally would have reacted to instantly and cleaned the bathroom with a cleaner that usually caused undue mental torment. Nothing happened.

Upon Dave's return, one of our daughters was in the hospital, and circumstances made it impossible for me to eat for a period of seven hours after getting up. Normally, I would have been passed out by then. God had healed not only the allergies, but the blood sugar problem as well! Since the night I asked God to touch my body, I have not had one reaction, even though I have been eating all my allergy foods. Once again I can eat normally!

Since then, self-discipline has become a way of life for me, though not without occasional struggle. Building a life characterized by self-discipline required making changes. Often we balk at the thought of making changes, even if we know they are good for us. Sometimes we aren't even aware of the rut we are in until the rut becomes so deep it seems as if we can never get out. This was the case with Louise.

Louise's Story

"I have always hated routines and schedules. I couldn't stand being bored; I lived on crisis and excitement. They even became my means of survival. At fifteen I left home and moved around a lot. My behavior was impulsive—I did what I felt like doing when I felt like doing it.

"If I had had self-discipline in high school, however, I could have avoided a lot of heartache. My boyfriend and I had set the date for our wedding. I didn't want to go through with it, but he said the invitations were sent and I couldn't back out. If I had had more control of my life, I could have called it off. That started the downward slide.

"I was rebelling against my parents' rigid, strict, organized life-style. Now I have been married five times, and after the last divorce two years ago I felt I couldn't go on. I felt worthless—a failure at everything. When I got depressed, I took the easy way out—I swallowed pills. When the going got tough, I walked out. I had used marriage as an escape, first from home, later from one bad situation to another. Each time it only got worse, and finally I got in over my head.

"When the last marriage fell apart, I went into a severe depression. My life was completely out of control, and I had no discipline whatsoever. A recent injury at work was aggravated by stress, causing me severe pain. When I would feel pain I reverted to the drugs. I didn't have control over so many things that I finally felt, 'What's the use of trying?' Hopelessness engulfed me, and I seriously considered suicide.

"Once, I was high on drugs and was riding my motorcycle when the police picked me up, impounded my motorcycle, and put me in the hospital. I overdosed again in the hospital and the doctors said that I had to have rehabilitation treatment before I could be released.

"My parents came all the way across the country to get me and take me to a rehabilitation hospital in my home town. One weekend, after I had been in the hospital about six weeks, my parents visited me and brought my four-year-old son with them. The drugs had taken their toll on my memory, and I didn't even recognize my son. I watched as they left my room and walked to the elevator. My son leaned against the wall at the end of the hall, his head in his arm, and sobbed. He loved me so much and wanted me to come home. I felt terrible! How low I was not even to be able to care for or remember my own son! I determined then and there to do something about it.

"I asked my parents if I could go to church with them the next Sunday. While there I asked the pastor to come visit me in the hospital. I thought he would forget, but he came the next morning and prayed with me. At that point I started to come back to reality.

"I was almost a vegetable from the drugs. It seemed hopeless. My mind was so messed up that I couldn't even remember who my doctor was, and I had been seeing him almost daily for over six weeks. I asked the nurses, cleaning staff, anyone who might know who my doctor was. Finally one nurse pointed him out to me. I went to him and explained that I was okay and ready to go home. But he said they had scheduled me for another electric shock treatment and I had to do that first before I could go home.

"I was *so* scared! It was awful! They had to strap me down. Afterward I had to stay for two weeks for observation. During that time I played the piano for hours in a small room. One patient would come in almost every day and visit with me. After my release, she sent me flowers. She said her whole family started to go to church and became Christians.

"It was hard for me when I went home. There were no support groups, and the church was small. I now see what my lifestyle has done to my son. He can't cope with stress, has little discipline, and runs from his problems like I used to.

"It's hard to think about five different marriages. But my last husband was really a wonderful guy. We may have been able to make it if I had been more disciplined, had not gotten angry so easily, had not become so defensive, and had taken the blame when I deserved it. If he saw things differently than I did, instead of working things out, I would go off and do my own thing. I was running away again.

"A couple in my church has shown me unconditional love. Knowing someone believes in me for who I am has helped me turn my life around. There are other ministries as well that have had a profound effect on my life.

"I have rededicated my life to the Lord and started putting my priorities in order. I put routines back into my life like devotions and exercise. I learned to love myself again and began to do things just for me instead of living only for my family. With professional help I took a walk back through my childhood and replayed all the garbage in my life. I took responsibility for my irresponsible behavior. It was exhausting and draining, but very freeing.

"Developing a personal relationship with Christ encourages me to discipline myself to spend time with Him. Christ has given me a new perspective on life, and with His help, I am gaining control over my physical pain through exercise and acceptance. Cutting down on my medications has helped me think more clearly; I'm more alert, vivacious, and confident. I am not so easily stressed out. This in turn affects the kind of mother I am.

"I love a clean, orderly house. And I love to entertain, but I was so embarrassed at the state of my house from not having the discipline to clean it, that I wouldn't have anyone over. I had isolated myself and become very lonely, and I am not the loner type. I was so down on myself that I didn't think anyone would like me. Lately, I have been reaching out to others and am starting to have people over again. It has given me a whole new purpose for my life.

"I am becoming healthier spiritually, physically, and emotionally. Friends and fellowship—especially with mature Christians who accept me and whose lives radiate love and the fruits of the Spirit—have changed my life!"

Judy's Story

"I was plunging farther into a dark hole, and I couldn't dig myself out. The faster I spun my wheels, the slower I seemed to go. I was out of control. The world was passing me by, and I was helpless to do anything about it. I hated myself. What was wrong with me? Discipline seemed to come naturally to my organized friends. Why couldn't I be like them?

"I felt unkempt and could never just be myself when someone came over, because I was always so embarrassed. I couldn't enjoy my friends' visits because I was on the defensive trying to justify my lack of discipline. I became critical of others as a result.

"One day in a television interview a lady was telling how she used to be a slob. She had no clean clothes and could never find what she was looking for. I thought she had been watching me! I also thought I would be like that the rest of my life. I didn't realize I had an option.

"The interview was at nine o'clock in the morning. By ten I was in the mall bookstore buying the last copy of the featured book. I sat in the mall reading that book. Then I went to Woolworth's, bought the listed supplies, and went home to de-junk my house.

"I went overboard and became very legalistic and a slave to my schedule, but I guess I needed to in order to find a balance. The whole process took about four months, but it has taken years to break the lifelong patterns of sloppiness I had developed. Because I am sanguine, I don't really care what I get done today — I know the work will always be there tomorrow.

"Self-discipline has given me peace of mind. Now I have the freedom to pursue other areas I have always wanted to explore. I have always enjoyed crafts, but I never had time for them because I was always digging for socks, papers, or other items. The cupboards were a mess, and the laundry was never done. Now I have more time to enjoy life and be with the kids.

"I remember what a neat feeling it was when I first became organized not having to clean house for two days before my mother could come over. I knew that if I could tackle the home organization area, I could do the same in other areas.

"Don't ever let someone say, 'That's just your nature.' It will take a conscious effort, but once you start you will see results. Discipline goes into our spiritual lives as well. How can you have a quiet spirit when there are one hundred million things staring you in the face? I think Satan uses disorganization to get our minds off things that are urgent."

Bruce's Story

"My lack of self-discipline has caused me to miss many opportunities. For me, self-discipline is planning. For a long time I balked at the idea of planning in any area because I felt it was the same as admitting that I didn't have control. I thought to be really in control I should be able to take things as they came. Now I realize that when I feel the most out of control and frustrated with myself is when I don't take the time to adequately plan.

"My lack of discipline has affected me mainly in two areas: eating and finances. Without self-discipline I couldn't reach or maintain my ideal weight. I would lose control and the domino effect would take over: 'I've gone this far—who cares now?' So, I would gain back ten pounds instead of five.

"Before I was a Christian, I would spend money on whatever I wanted. I had plenty of money, but because I didn't plan a budget or balance my checkbook, I got into trouble. At the end of the month I would have nothing left. I wasted about 90 percent of my money.

"When I became a Christian I had to quit my job, since it was not a God-honoring occupation. The first things that God convicted me of were my lack of discipline in the areas of eating, finances, and relationships. I went cold turkey. I dropped all my friends and had to find two jobs working sixteen hours a day to pay for my lack of discipline. I really paid my dues for that one!

"Also, I couldn't deny my gluttony any longer. It was coming between me and the Lord. I wasn't successful in gaining control at first. It took a couple of months. I sought out books on self-discipline and read about fifteen different ones to get information on each area. It drove me batty.

"Through the years I have developed a daily commitment to self-discipline, but my success comes through the Lord. At first, I didn't praise the Lord for my success or give Him the credit. But now I know I will always have the tendency to lack self-control. I know, too, that I don't have to work at it alone. The Lord keeps me.

"A lack of self-discipline caused me to beat myself up a lot: 'You'll always be late; unorganized; overweight.' I didn't even try because I knew I could never succeed.

"The benefits of self-discipline for me have been noticeable. I got out of debt and now maintain a weight thirty pounds lighter. And now failure is a way of learning for the next time—it doesn't crush me any more.

"Spiritually, I depend on the Lord. I always saw dependency as an unhealthy thing, but now I realize that being self-disciplined is being totally dependent on God. It brings me joy and enhances my whole self-image."

From My Own Archives

The jungle was like the Garden of Eden, beautiful in its lushness, variety, and color scheme, alive with the ferociousness of untamed beasts, both man and animal. The sun would rise methodically at six o'clock in the morning and set just as methodically at six in the evening throughout the year. We were located in Zaire, Africa, only a few degrees from the equator, at a high enough elevation to enjoy a perfect climate year round. My husband was a bush pilot, flying supplies, missionaries, medicine, mail, and patients to various outstations.

For a time I would get up every morning at 4:30 while the masses still slept. In my ignorance and innocence, I would trek daily up a fairly steep mountain. Clothes soaked from the very early morning dew on shoulder-high elephant grass, I would continue on until I reached my favorite spot. From this point, I could see almost 360 degrees to the surrounding valleys below and the fruitful mountain ranges in the distance. I would reach the top of the mountain just in time to see an exquisite sunrise. There I would get to know God more intimately as a friend and as my heavenly Father.

When daylight was full upon me, it was time to go. I hated to come down from the mountain. I knew that when I reached the bottom, the problems of the day would overwhelm me. But I also knew that if I hadn't spent time alone with God, I would lack the strength to cope with the problems and temptations of the day. The walk back was sometimes discouraging. With every step down the mountain, my heart would become heavier until I began to consciously draw upon the riches that were mine in Jesus Christ.

One day some missionary friends cautioned me not to go up the mountain in the dark. There were wild dogs, snakes, and madmen with machetes eager to pounce upon unsuspecting souls. At first, my desire for the mountaintop meeting with God each morning was greater than my fear of the unknown. But with each passing day the climb up the mountain became less joyful and more fearful. I would cringe at every rustle of leaves or every faint animal call, lest I be overtaken by some unwanted tragedy.

Finally, my fear won out, and I completely abandoned my morning mountain climbs. Instead, I went down into the valley to the grass airstrip and jogged the length of the strip to watch the sunrise from there. It was also beautiful, but not nearly as impressive.

It was a risk going to the mountaintop, but the effort afforded a rich payment. There was no risk in the valley. It was safe and secure.

But I wonder, if I could do it over again, would it not be worth the trouble to overcome my fears in exchange for the majesty of the mountaintop sunrises? Or would I again take the easy and secure way of viewing the same sunrise, but enjoy only a mediocre view in comparison?

The analogy may hold true for you. Your risk may involve letting go of the mediocre, secure, and unfruitful in exchange for the excitement, riches, and perhaps sufferings of Jesus Christ.

During our term in Africa, through temptations, struggles, and fears, I came to the very end of my human strength and resources. It was a very difficult time, but in the end a very rewarding one, for only when my own resources were depleted could I fully understand that in me dwelleth no good thing.

I was trying to live the Christian life in my own power and strength. There is an end to human strength, but there is no end to God's strength. Struggles on foreign soil are much more acute, much more magnified. One can't drown them out by television, activities, or material possessions. In the jungle I was isolated together with my struggles. I had to face them head on; I could not run away from them or ignore them and hope they would go away.

Growth hurts. When we come to the point where we welcome pain and sorrow to the same extent that we welcome joy and happiness, then we know God has been working in our lives. We recognize pain and sorrow as the very elements that God often uses to draw us closer to Himself.

I have failed in many ways over the years, and through my failures God has become more precious to me. Yet, I have also been very successful in those tasks God has called me to do. I am confident because my resources come from God Himself.

What about you? Are you willing to invest thirty minutes a day to become successful in those tasks God has called you to do? You may need to redefine your present concept of success, but it will be success nonetheless. Our responsibility is to be faithful and build on the life God has given us.

This step-by-step plan will guide you in developing self-discipline so that you may be able to reach your God-given potential. If you can commit thirty minutes a day, you will begin to enjoy the benefits of a more disciplined life.

While I was visiting a town in another state, a woman begged me to carve out some time for her friend who was so overwhelmed by the disorganization in her home that she had almost ceased to function as a person. Although I was scheduled to leave the next day, I agreed. The friend was quite nervous on my arrival. There were boxes, paper, and mounds of junk piled higher than my head. A thin pathway curved through the junk leading from room to room. There were no clean dishes and you couldn't even find the dining room table. Of all the homes I had organized over the years, this was the worst. But there was hope even in that situation.

Even after working together for about six hours, we had only finished one corner of the living room. We had cleared off the couch and end tables. My parting instructions to her were, "Even if you spend only thirty minutes a day chipping away at the mountain of disorganization, eventually you will have gone through the whole house. However, if you *don't* spend that time, a year from now your house can only be worse."

I say the same to you — by chipping away at your lack of discipline, you will be closer to becoming what God wants you to be. And, if you *don't* spend that time, a year from now your life will have remained status quo, not having gone beyond mediocrity and possibly mere existence. This book is only one way to help you become more disciplined. Maybe you have found others or you are already disciplined. Great! Come along with us and pat yourself on the back — maybe you will even gain some new insights. God's best to each of you as you embark on this challenging endeavor!

PART ONE

PREREQUISITES FOR PROFICIENT SELF-DISCIPLINE

PERSPECTIVE ON
A PRECEPT

For some years Alex had struggled with several areas of his life that he knew did not glorify God. His sexual desires were manifested in unhealthy ways, food and alcohol cravings kept him overweight and sluggish, and a general lack of discipline prevented him from accomplishing much of anything.

Alex felt as if he were in a battle of wills—his against his. Now how can that be? He *wanted* to live a life pleasing to the Lord. Yes, he had recognized his need for Jesus Christ to forgive his sin and had consequently acknowledged Him as his personal Savior. So, why was he still struggling?

Paul accentuates this personal battle:

I do not understand what I do. For what I want to do I do not do, but what I hate I do. And if I do what I do not want to do, I agree that the law is good. As it is, it is no longer I myself who do it, but it is sin living in me. I know that nothing good lives in me, that is, in my sinful nature. For I have the desire to do what is good, but I cannot carry it out. For what I do is not the good I want to do; no, the evil I do not want to do—this I keep on doing. Now if I do what I do not want to do, it is no longer I who do it, but it is sin living in me that does it.

So I find this law at work: When I want to do good, evil is right there with me. For in my inner being I delight in God's law, but I see another law at work in the members of my body, waging war against the law of my mind and making me a prisoner of the law of sin at work within my members. What a wretched man I am! Who will rescue me from this body of death? Thanks be to God — through Jesus Christ our Lord!

So then, I myself in my mind am a slave to God's law, but in the sinful nature a slave to the law of sin. (Romans 7:15–25)

What does this mean for Alex? Can he therefore give no thought to his actions and just let his flesh carry him where it will? Does he have a responsibility to enact God's plan for his life, or is he completely at the mercy of his circumstances and environment?

Only the Holy Spirit of God can change our hearts. Though we can change outwardly, we depend on the Holy Spirit to mold us and make us into the likeness of Jesus Christ (see 2 Corinthians 3:18). But because God has given us minds that enable us to understand, hearts that enable us to desire, and wills that enable us to make choices, we have the ability to respond to or reject God's work in us.

We are urged in 1 Timothy 4:7 to train ourselves to be godly. That takes diligence on our part. And the writer of Hebrews says, "Make every effort to live in peace with all men and to be holy" (Hebrews 12:14). That takes work and perseverance from us.

How, then, can we do this? By striving harder and harder, purely through self-effort? No. We are dependent upon God for the power to do what He requires of us. Ours is the conscious choice to recognize and submit to that dependence, draw upon it in the time of need, and then bring it full circle in praise of God for the enablement.

Self-discipline is a mutual effort between the indwelling Holy Spirit and the will of one who is yielded to God's authority. It involves mastering our attitudes, emotions, and actions. With the help of the Holy Spirit and the Word of God, we can develop godly motives, believing that God loves us and wants His best for us (and sometimes His best is very different from what we envision it to be). Then we can activate a plan to bring our desires in tune with God's desires for us (see Psalm 40:5).

Self-control is a fruit of the Spirit (see Galatians 5:22-23). It involves abstaining from what may be good in order to enjoy that which is best. It includes authentic living and breaking the chains of habit that threaten to strangle us. It focuses on exercising restraint in our actions and feelings.

Self-discipline gives direction, helps us to live productive lives, and gives us the courage to stand by our convictions. It involves training ourselves to produce self-control in a specific area. Because self-control and self-discipline are so similar, we will use the terms interchangeably.

With self-discipline we channel our efforts toward a purpose instead of stumbling through life with no thought as to how to live it. Self-discipline helps us do God's will. It is a positive self-denial where we say no to our flesh and yes to God (see Matthew 16:24). "For the grace of God that brings salvation has appeared to all men. It teaches us to say 'No' to ungodliness and worldly passions, and to live self-controlled, upright and godly lives in this present age, while we wait for the blessed hope—the glorious appearing of our great God and Savior, Jesus Christ" (Titus 2:11-13).

Our self-control is a gift from God. He has given us the resources and power to say no to sin, but we have to appropriate them for ourselves. Sometimes the struggle between our will and God's will can be intense. The truth of God's Word sets us free to obey the promptings of the Spirit. Self-control is Spirit control.

Self-discipline is not an end unto itself but a means of bringing glory to God. Through self-discipline we develop godly habits— habits that begin in the heart. Our habits will either help us to flee temptation and live godly lives, or they will keep us in bondage to our sinful desires, causing us to fall short of all that we could be in Jesus Christ.

God accepts us unconditionally. Therefore, we are not intent on increasing our self-discipline for the purpose of becoming more worthy to God, but rather to make full use of the resources God has entrusted to us. Self-discipline helps us to define our priorities, determine our boundaries, and develop our potential.

Therefore, prepare your minds for action; be self-controlled.
(1 Peter 1:13)

Be self-controlled and alert. Your enemy, the devil, prowls around like a roaring lion looking for someone to devour. Resist him, standing firm in the faith. (1 Peter 5:8–9; see also 1 Thessalonians 5:6, 8; Titus 2:2, 5–6)

For Alex and those of us like him, harmony between self-control and God's control is possible. But it won't be easy. It is my hope that the following chapters will give you insight as to how to cooperate with God, allowing Him to develop self-discipline in your life.

TWO

PLAN YOUR LIFE
WITH A PURPOSE

Have you ever felt like you were just existing, like you were not sure where you were really going? Have you ever reached one goal, only to wonder *What now?* while blindly making your way through the next months or years?

During the first nine years of our marriage we had only one goal: to train for the foreign mission field. First, there was a two-year stint in the Navy with assignments overseas and in various states. Then came years of school which taught us lessons that couldn't be learned in a classroom — lessons about life, about God, and about people.

Finally, we were ready to apply to a mission.

Our time of candidacy — an in-depth evaluation by the mission — and subsequent acceptance was followed by a year of deputation — the securing of promised funds for our term overseas. A year in Switzerland learning French fulfilled our language requirements. Then we returned to the States for orientation — that last bit of intense training before the mission sends you on your way. At last the day for our departure arrived. With three children and overloaded suitcases, we began our trip to Zaire, Africa.

After an arduous three-day trip, we finally reached our destination in the jungle. Those who had already spent years away from their homeland welcomed us with excitement. Gradually, we adjusted to the new smells, sights, sounds, and ways of living in a different culture, and life settled into somewhat of a routine.

But after a number of months of this routine, though completely enjoyable in itself, I started to feel as if I were just standing still, going nowhere—as if I were merely acting out a script with no input on my part. Nine years of being caught up in the goal of serving on the mission field had given us a vision—a corporate striving for a specific result. We worked, struggled, and sacrificed together to make that dream a reality.

Arriving in Zaire meant that our goal had ceased to exist to a certain extent. But surely reaching one aspiration didn't mean there were no more mountains to climb or rivers to cross! Where was my vision for the future? Was I really all that I could be? Proverbs 29:18 says that without a vision the people perish.

The "Think-Out"

My frustration over this mere existence increased, so I determined to do something about it. For one whole day I shut myself in my bedroom with my typewriter while Dave took care of the girls. During that intense period of evaluation, prayer, planning, and dreaming, I came up with a set of guidelines that have served me well over the years.

Since I developed my original plan, I have re-evaluated annually, and I am often surprised how much of what I want to accomplish, or to become, actually transpires—sometimes without any conscious effort on my part! I have found that, as I write down my plans, I subconsciously make decisions that unite me with my goals.

I call this plan my "think-out." This was before the market became saturated with books on goals and life planning, so at the time the concept was more revolutionary than it is now.

To my amazement, after almost one year to the day the feelings of frustration started to creep up again. I re-evaluated, keeping many of my original goals, revising others, eliminating still others, and adding new ones. By writing down my aspirations, I freed my mind from cumbersome thoughts and was able to concentrate on those areas I considered most important.

I have taught seminars on time management in various communities, and the foundational material is always a personal think-out such as the one I developed in Africa years ago. As a result of sharing this plan, lives have been changed, directions altered, aspirations fulfilled, and a sense of enjoyment for life renewed.

Holly

Holly was a befuddled mess on the verge of calling it quits when I met her. Each failure only confirmed her desire to give up permanently. Life was hopeless, and she was useless. In desperation she asked if I would help. She would give life one more try.

Holly's recent commitment to rekindle her walk with the Lord allowed her to overcome the otherwise insurmountable odds. First, Holly worked on her personal think-out to give us an idea how to proceed. A modified think-out with her answers follows. How would *you* answer these questions?

Holly started by asking God to help her formulate the ideas He wanted her to have and to discover the path He wanted her to follow.

1. Determine your philosophy of life. Who are you? What is your reason for being? The happiest people are those who seem to have a purpose for living—a cause, a higher calling—that beckons them through all of life, come what may.

Holly wrote, "I am venturing on a path leading heavenward, so that at my destination I am Christlike in all I do, say, and think. Each day draws me closer to being conformed to His image. Every trial and setback gives opportunity for showing God's power through it. Every joy and pleasure are used to bring glory to Him.

"I am on a journey with a Friend. By the end of the journey I will know this Friend completely and He will know me. We will be of like mind, purpose, and countenance. Why? So that His name may be praised."

2. If you could do anything in the world regardless of money, circumstances, or people, what would you do? If you could be anything you wanted to be, what would you be like?

Holly based her life desires on Colossians 1:10–19:

- Live a life worthy of the Lord.
- Please Him in every way.
- Bear fruit in every good work.
- Grow in the knowledge of God.
- Be strengthened with all power that:
  - I may have great patience and endurance.
  - I may joyfully give thanks for everything to the Father.

Then, in describing the kind of person she would be if she
could, Holly wrote, "As a creation of God, I would like to reflect the
glory of God in my actions, countenance, spirit, thoughts, and
desires. I would like to accept my husband totally, dwelling on his
virtues. I need to admire him and be a reflection of his good image
of himself.

"I need to build him up, encourage him, and help him to believe
he can become a man of God, full of the joy of the Lord. I would
like to be a wife my husband can trust—richly satisfying his needs. I
want to help him, not hinder him, all the days of his life. I want to
be a woman of prayer, knowing the power of God and seeing His
power work out answers to prayer. I want to be a woman of strength,
dignity, and love, reaching out to the hurt and downcast, bringing
joy to all I meet. I want to reflect the glory of God!

"My mother role would see a change. I would be available, interested in even the smallest tidbit my daughters share with me.
When I speak, my words would be kind and wise. I would build in
my children a healthy self-image—one where they have the freedom to love themselves and accept love freely from others, so in
turn they can impart love to all they meet.

"I would have a happy and joyful countenance so that daily my
children would see the love of Jesus in me. I would encourage them
at every turn so that their potential would crystallize into all that
God meant it to be.

"My children would see my love for God and His love for them
through me. They would see the validity of prayer and the impor-

tance of it. They would, as a result of my life, desire to know God more fully.

"I would take time for my children and experience with them the joys and sorrows, excitements and disappointments, strivings and accomplishments of life.

"My home would be known as a haven of rest to the weary, a place of healing for the hurt, and a well of joy to the downcast. My husband and children would rise up and call me blessed!"

3. What are your most important personal needs? We often feel unfulfilled because we ignore basic needs that are unique to us, taking into account our personality and temperament.

A few of the needs Holly listed in each area are:

Mental
- I need to be organized (it helps my life go smoother).
- I need to be creative and to dream (it adds enrichment to my life).
- I need to use and stimulate my mind (it stretches me).

Physical
- I need to enjoy nature (it offers peace).
- I need adventure (it adds zest to life).
- I need to be physically fit (it makes me feel good).
- I need variety in my work (it keeps me interested).

Emotional
- I need to love and be loved (it's foundational).
- I need challenges (they motivate me).
- I need a certain amount of independence (it gives me control).
- I need to be spontaneous (it makes life more fun).

Other
- I need to teach (it's my contribution to humanity).
- I need to write (it is an extension of myself).
- I need to positively influence others (it gives me meaning).

Holly went through the process of allowing God to infiltrate each area of her life. With His help she clarified her priorities and discovered more about the person God made her to be.

This is a book about self-discipline. It doesn't matter how much self-discipline we have if we don't know where we are going or if we are going in the wrong direction. By formulating a life plan, you can pinpoint your efforts to develop self-discipline in the areas that matter the most to you.

THREE

PRIORITIES
IN PRACTICE

Holly began to eliminate anything in her life that did not fit in with her life purpose—friends who kept pulling her down; destructive soap operas that left her depressed and discontented; the food gorging that sometimes seemed to consume her life; and the self-made obligations that held no real interest for her.

It was not easy at first for Holly to let go of her familiar lifestyle. There was a certain security in wrapping the intimacy of the known, however malevolent it might be, around her. But once Holly garnered the courage to begin letting go, she relished a new-found freedom that overshadowed any loss she might have felt.

As a result of answering the questions on her think-out, Holly defined her life purpose, discovered what kind of person she would like to be, and decided which needs were most important to her. Next, she began to work out a personal program to reach the aspirations she had outlined. In doing so, she found it necessary to determine her priorities within each area of her life.

Holly divided her life into several areas and made a general statement about her desires for each area. Since she had already thought through the kind of person she would like to become, this step was more a matter of organizing her desires based on her answers to the previous questions.

- Spiritual: Cultivate a growing, vitalizing, and powerful relationship with the Lord.
- Marriage: Develop a close, loving relationship with my husband that enables him to be free to express his innermost dreams, fears, and thoughts.
- Children: Nurture happy, well-adjusted children who enjoy life and appreciate and love their family.
- Home: Create a home known for its joy, hospitality, and order.
- Personal: Develop and maintain an energetic and healthy body. Expand as a person socially and intellectually through nurturing interests in various fields.
- Career: Follow God's leading in a career path that uses the talents and abilities He has given.

Then Holly outlined specific steps she would need to take in order to attain her desires in each area. Holly's plan made her desires attainable and measurable. For instance, her plan for reaching her spiritual desire included:

- Get up an hour earlier for a time of prayer and Bible reading.
- Read a spiritual emphasis book once a week.
- Listen to a spiritual emphasis tape once a week.
- Share how the Lord has worked in my life with one person each week.
- Memorize and apply one verse of Scripture every day.
- Fast one day a week.

Next, Holly thought about all of her obligations as well as the things that she felt other people wanted her to do. She considered each item and, if it fit her life purpose and was something she felt God wanted her to do, she placed it on one of two lists. The most important items with the highest priority went on her "A" list, and those which should or could be done sometime in the future, but were not pressing, she placed on her "B" list.

Her prioritizing completed, Holly made up both a weekly to-do list and a daily to-do list with some built-in flexibility. Systematically, she reviewed each goal and determined what she needed to do either weekly or daily in order to accomplish it.

Her faithfulness in completing the daily and weekly lists would allow her to reach her goals. In turn, she would become the person she felt God would have her become. Not that at each stage she wasn't pleasing the Lord, but she realized that if she didn't move forward, she would stagnate and vegetate.

Now Holly's metamorphosis did not happen in a few weeks or even a few months. The process is an ongoing one of ever reaching, ever becoming. Nor does she always complete her daily and weekly lists. There are bum days when she abandons her lists entirely and days when circumstances supersede any plans she may have had. But Holly is moving forward with a purpose, and that has made all the difference in her life!

Moving Forward with a Purpose

Yes, we can be content in who we are now, but who we are today may not be what we should be tomorrow. As we stretch, we grow and mature. And as we grow and mature, we appreciate and experience life more fully.

When setting goals, we need to ask ourselves if they bring glory to God. In order for our lives to glorify God, our goals need to reflect that same purpose. God has planned our days in advance, and it is our responsibility to superimpose our plans with His (see Psalm 139:15-16).

Now I realize there are several excellent books that hold to the thinking that all of our life belongs to God and we should honor God in each area of our life. Therefore, we should not give one area priority over another. I disagree to a certain extent, because the spiritual aspect of my life *is* the most important. From it all others have their being.

Moreover, in making wise decisions I place my family before my career and my marriage before my friends. When conflicting concerns arise, I have already determined my higher priority, and I can be confident that I am proceeding in the right direction. My pre-determined priorities eliminate indecision.

We will never be able to do all that others think we should do, or even all that we may like to do. But if we channel our energies in the right direction, we should be able to accomplish that which is most important. Jesus Christ did not heal all the sick, nor feed all the hungry, yet he could say to His Father, "I have brought you glory on earth by completing the work you gave me to do" (John 17:4).

That is all God requires of each of us — not to do someone else's work but to do what God has planned for *us*. And that brings us back to the importance of having a personal blueprint — to knowing our direction and pursuing it.

Once we have determined God's purpose for our life, defined our priorities and goals, and developed a plan to accomplish them, we will need to keep up with our plans. We need a system to help keep us on track and navigate us toward accomplishing our daily, weekly, and monthly goals.

One such efficient system is a notebook planner. The notebook can help you discipline yourself to do the tasks which you have chosen, and it will save you time. For every half-hour you spend planning, you will save hours in effort during the week.

Your loose-leaf notebook can be any size that fits your style. I like a small one that fits into my purse, and Dave's fits neatly into a suit pocket. Today's market offers many tools to make it easy to keep our lives in order. A few of the following suggestions may get you started in organizing your notebook.

Designate sections that will include these areas:

Goals. A written statement of your objective in each area of your life. Included are the measurable steps you have developed previously.

Monthly Calendar. A master calendar where you will schedule commitments and appointments and note birthdays, anniversaries, and family activities.

Weekly and/or Daily Calendar. Enables you to schedule in projects during blocks of free time. The daily calendar will be your to-do list and will include appointments, projects, errands, and phone calls.

Project Section. Much of what we do in our lives comes under the heading "Project." Improving our cooking, applying for a job, getting the car ready to sell, or sprucing up the outside of the house are projects because they involve several steps. Make a separate page for each project and list the steps needed to complete it.

To-Do List. Unlike the project section, this master list includes everything you can probably accomplish in less than an hour. Typical to-do lists might include writing your friend a thank you note, mending your husband's jacket, taking your wife out to dinner, washing the car, checking into gymnastics for your daughter, or returning your friend's book. You can further dissect your to-do list by having two pages — one each for "A" and "B" items.

Address and Telephone Directory. It will be handy and at your fingertips. It is especially helpful if you are out and need the information.

Shopping Section. On my shopping page I have a section for each store I shop at regularly. One may be for office supplies, another for clothes, and another for groceries. Then, if I am in the neighborhood, I can stop at the respective store and pick up the items I need without wasting a trip.

Enter your grocery or other items as you think of them. It works well for me to stay one ahead of everything I typically use: paper towels, toothpaste, applesauce, ketchup, printer ribbons, copy paper, or pencils. As I open a new item, I immediately jot it down on my grocery list so that I always have a backup. In this way I eliminate unnecessary trips to the store because I ran out of some things. Even if you buy in quantity, eventually you will need replacements. I also keep a typed master list of all my grocery items and give it a quick glance before leaving the store to jog my memory.

Create your notebook according to your individual lifestyle, and make it work for you. After one of my clients learned to use the notebook system, she expressed how much smoother her life had become, how many more things she was able to accomplish, and how much more confident she felt knowing she was moving forward with a purpose. Setting up her notebook was a continuing process that we fine-tuned over the course of several weeks, adding some sections and deleting others.

One day I found this message from a friend on my answering machine: "I just made out my *first* weekly schedule. Aren't you *proud* of me or *what!?* I'm really excited to get all the principles into my life. It seems I do it one at a time, but at least I'm getting there!"

Planning, thinking, and organizing help us to discover and fulfill our unique purpose. Planning enables us to embrace a divine perspective; we retain control under the authority of God, increase our productivity for the glory of God, and reduce our stress through the enjoyment of God. Even Jesus followed a divine schedule (see John 7:1-8; 12:23, 27; Galatians 4:4).

Time Management Tips

The following list of time management tips for today's lifestyle may help you conquer a convicting condition. Or it may disclose a delightful discovery:

- Eliminate anything that does not move you in the direction you have determined God wants you to go.
- Set goals that will open new doors and that you can visualize yourself achieving.
- Set realistic deadlines and allow adequate time to meet them.
- Set a daily standard schedule to eliminate repetitive thinking. For instance, I usually do laundry, iron, and bake bread on Mondays; clean and swim on Tuesdays; schedule appointments for Wednesday; swim on Thursdays; and run errands and do grocery shopping on Fridays. From there I plan my schedule, allowing several hours each day for writing, research, or completing other projects.
- Break projects down into manageable steps. Focus on one step at a time and it won't seem so overwhelming.
- Reward your successes.
- Get up one-half to one hour earlier. When the ladies in a ten-week time management course followed through on this assignment, one lady returned the next week with this report: "I got so much done in the mornings that I would just walk around and wait for everyone else to get up."

- Be conscious of a ministry of interruptions. God is ultimately in control of your schedule. Appreciate certain interruptions as coming from Him for your good and for His glory.

- Buy only that which enhances your priorities. Anything else will just be a waste of money and clutter up your life.

- Learn to enjoy the moments of your day — smell the flowers, listen to the birds, appreciate a child's smile, feel the sun's warmth. Plan for relaxation and fun time and for time alone each day.

- Eliminate time wasters — too much television, telephone, shopping, junk mail, unnecessary meetings.

- Write down thoughts immediately in your notebook — an errand that needs to be run, an idea you may want to act on, a reminder for one of your children.

- Take advantage of moods, energy levels, and cycles — times of year, days of month, hours in a day.

- Do what is most important first, even if it is unpleasant.

- Allow time to invest in the people the Lord has reserved for you.

- Learn to delegate. Consider Jethro, who encouraged Moses to delegate some of his authority and let others help judge disputes (see Exodus 18:14–23).

Sometimes we miss out on meaningful opportunities because we have consistently made poor choices, because we are not prepared, or because we would rather take the easy road through life. Dave says that most people don't see a reason for something until the reason is on their doorstep, and then it is too late.

I received my first rejection slip from a publication over twenty years ago. During the last two decades I have not been sitting idly by. I have tried to prepare for God's timing concerning my writing. Through the years I have encountered many obstacles and necessary divergents. But I knew the time would come. I continued to learn writing techniques, read hundreds of books in various fields, and pursued habits of excellence in the areas that God had for me at the time. Being ready for opportunities takes self-discipline.

Self-discipline enables us to do God's will and to be faithful stewards of our time, intellect, abilities, and resources. Perhaps you are not quite sure how to pursue an interest you feel is from the

Lord. Begin by seeking information relating to your objective. Choose good role models. Ask questions and listen to the answers. Consult with experts in the field of your interest. Study people who have lost the battle and learn from them.

Trevor was interested in repairing bicycles and wanted to own his own bike shop some day. Although he had a good job, it had ceased to challenge him. In following his dream, Trevor studied bike repair manuals from the local library. He made friends with a bike shop owner who took him on as an apprentice in Trevor's spare time. Several months later, Trevor felt he had enough information to open a small shop in his own garage with the other shop owner's blessing. As his expertise grew, so did his clientele, until one day he was able to sever the security of his old job.

Why Do We Do What We Do?

We do what we do for several reasons. Habits, whether good or bad, become so ingrained in us that we often act mindlessly, giving no thought to the eventual consequences. We can form habits deliberately, but more often we form them by default—we take the path of least resistance and "go with the flow." If we take that path often enough, it will become a habit.

Originally, our actions may result from trying to gain control of our circumstances, environment, possessions, or the people around us. We think that controlling these areas more tightly will satisfy and fulfill us. But we jeopardize our health, our values, and our relationships in the fight to gain control.

Jesus never ran to and fro, forcing the pieces to fit and struggling to control all that touched His life, even in urgent times. We, on the other hand, try to manufacture our worth by being more and more in control. A certain amount of control over ourselves is necessary, but we must first yield ourselves to the living God so that our motive in desiring control is to glorify God, not to measure our self-worth.

Perhaps we are responding to the demands of others. Again, we often thoughtlessly acquiesce to people and circumstances because we have not determined with God the path He would have us follow.

Some people continuously act on impulse, grabbing at whatever seems attractive at the moment. Now some spontaneity is healthy, but when we face all of life with a senseless striving to satisfy our impulses, we defeat ourselves.

Sometimes we do what we do to escape what we perceive to be more threatening, demanding, or painful. We may put up with a dirty house because it is unpleasant to wash the kitchen floor, or we may avoid working out conflicts because it is painful to face our weaknesses.

We need to make conscious decisions in order to change. Our aim is to develop godly habits that result in godly living. A habit is an established pattern of behavior. Research has shown that it takes about twenty-one days of repetition for an action to develop into a habit.

In order to reach this aim, we will need to take purposeful steps in that direction, and this often requires us to make changes. Sometimes we resist. Change often brings stress, fear, a sense of loss, and feelings of insecurity. Change awakens deep-seated emotional responses that may have lain dormant for years.

It takes courage to change. Our forty-plus moves in the last twenty years have offered countless opportunities for change. Most we met with excitement and expectancy. Some we resisted and finally gave in to. Some were inconsequential; others were major. We have learned that, on a human level, only change itself is certain. If that is the case, then it would be to our advantage to learn how to deal with change and glean the blessings afforded along the way.

On the positive side, change challenges our character and emboldens our thirst for life. We are stretched, tried, and proven through change. We are also blessed, satisfied, and encouraged because of change. Our perspective often determines if change will be debilitating or heartening, a springboard for growth or a pit for decay.

Making Wise Decisions

Decisions are a fact of life, whether by design or default. When we make decisions in response to feelings or appetites rather than divine direction, we often bring ourselves calamity. It is our responsibility as Christians to make wise decisions based on the teachings of Scripture, the guidance of the Holy Spirit, and the example of Jesus Christ.

God has created our minds to make decisions logically. The following steps may help give you direction for proceeding on the path God would have you take.

Consider all relevant information. Proverbs 19:2 warns us, "It is not good to have zeal without knowledge, nor to be hasty and miss the way." Define the real issue.

Review the alternatives. Ask yourself, "How would so-and-so solve this problem?" Which alternatives are the most consistent with your personal philosophy? Analyze the repercussions of each alternative. What are the consequences? "The wisdom of the prudent is to give thought to their ways, but the folly of fools is deception" (Proverbs 14:8; see also Luke 14:28–32). A sample chart is included at the end of the chapter to help you formulate a plan for making wise decisions based on your alternatives and priorities.

Seek counsel if necessary. By virtue of our human limitations, we cannot always have the insight necessary in considering all of our alternatives. "Plans fail for lack of counsel, but with many advisers they succeed" (Proverbs 15:22).

Trust God for the wisdom to make the right decision. "If any of you lacks wisdom, he should ask God, who gives generously to all without finding fault, and it will be given to him" (James 1:5).

Leave the results with God. When we make decisions in light of eternity, we will be successful, though not always in the way we view success. "In his heart a man plans his course, but the Lord determines his steps" (Proverbs 16:9).

God gives a supernatural peace (Philippians 4:7) that often affirms our right choices. We must also remember that God's timing may differ from ours. The need for decisions made on the basis of impulse is far less than our responsibility to adequately and intelligently consider the alternatives. As we seek to make decisions God's way, we will have a relaxed spirit of inner tranquillity.

Decision Making Alternatives

Make a chart modeled after the "Decision Making Alternatives" chart below, inserting your own items for the examples:

a. On the top row, write out your alternatives.

b. In the left column, list your priorities and assign each priority a value (how important is it to you?). With 1 as the lowest and 5 as the highest, circle the appropriate value rating for each priority.

c. Then rate how closely each alternative meets the rating for your priorities.

d. Add the numbers in each column. The alternative with the highest total will often come closest to fulfilling your goals.

Decision Making Alternatives

Alternatives ➡ Priorities ⬇	Teach a Sunday school class 1._____	Volunteer at crisis pregnancy center 2._____	Part-time job lecturing 3._____
1. To use gifts 1 2 3 4 ⑤	No patience with little ones ①	Have empathy ⑤	Speak well ⑤
2. To enjoy what I'm doing 1 2 3 ④ 5	Don't really enjoy teaching ①	Enjoy helping and contact with hurting people ⑤	I love the whole scenario ⑤
3. To make money 1 ② 3 4 5	Volunteer ①	Volunteer ①	Good pay ⑤
4. To have adequate time for my family 1 2 3 4 ⑤	A few hours a week ④	Would take too much time ①	Would take a big chunk of time ①
TOTALS	⑦	⑫	★ ⑯

PART TWO

RELATING SELF-DISCIPLINE TO THE WHOLE PERSON

FOUR

DEVELOPING PHYSICAL SELF-DISCIPLINE

She was overweight and undernourished, slovenly dressed, lacked adequate energy to meet an average day's demands, and was easily irritated at people and circumstances in general and herself in particular. Her name was Nelly. The kids in school used to chant behind her back, "Nelly, Nelly's made of jelly. Better not choose her, she's a loser!"

But Nelly sincerely wanted to better herself, to change, to become all that God wanted her to become. Only she had no idea where to begin. Undisciplined habits ran rampant in her family. In fact, as the youngest, Nelly was a composite of all the family members' worst habits. There are scores of Nellys in our neighborhoods, cities, and offices. Is there hope for the Nellys of America? Absolutely!

Suppose you had come to me for help in becoming more disciplined physically. How would I begin to train you? Since I am not there to advise you in person, walk with me through this chapter and imagine having your own personal instructor to coach you, encourage you, and hold you accountable.

"Oh, No! Anything but That!"

First, dig up a notebook or pad of paper to record where you are now, your path along the way, and your eventual success in developing physical self-discipline. On the first page write "Early Rising Time." Then for the next several months keep track of what time you get up. Begin by getting up a half-hour earlier tomorrow.

About twelve years ago I made a conscious decision to develop more self-discipline. The logical initial step was to get up earlier. I started with a half-hour, which at that time made it 5:30 in the morning. Still vivid in my mind is the difficulty with which I turned off the alarm and forced myself to put one foot on the floor. As I did so, I kept saying to myself over and over, "I am developing self-discipline."

No, it's not easy. But I can confidently say that it *does* get easier. Now, I wake up without an alarm around 3:30 in the morning, and from force of habit I jump out of bed before I have a chance to determine if I feel like it or not (except sometimes when Dave is out of town and I work into the wee hours of the night).

Much has been said about abiding by our natural time clocks, about taking advantage of the energy highs in being a morning or evening person, and about going with the flow of our body rhythms. That is true to a certain extent. (In fact, we will be talking about cycles and energy levels later in this chapter.) But much of our personal energy system can be affected by our habits, lifestyle, and level of commitment.

By nature, I am probably a night person. My parents are night people. They have their own business next to their home and normally work from noon to two or four in the morning, especially during busy seasons. There are advantages to working in the quiet hours after midnight — no disturbances, a sense of peace, hours of concentrated effort.

Nevertheless, most people will benefit by getting up earlier, not just for the extra time, but for the practice of self-discipline so that discipline will come more easily in other areas.

Maybe you'll be able to get up earlier only one day next week, but the next week you might make it three. The following week you might slip back to two and perhaps manage three again after that.

The point is to make progress. Discipline builds upon discipline. Each success encourages another. Pretty soon getting up early four days a week will be standard and painless.

After you have mastered getting up earlier five days a week, try perhaps forty-five minutes earlier once or twice a week. (If you implement the rest of the steps to developing physical self-discipline, you will find that you don't need as much sleep, and the sleep you do get will be more refreshing.) It's amazing how much more you can accomplish in that one-half to one hour in the morning. And it has been said that every hour of sleep before midnight is worth two after midnight.

Short naps in the afternoon improve our moods and level of alertness. They help us start fresh with renewed energy. They allow for relaxation amidst the stresses of a typical day.

"I Figured You'd Get to That!"

The next thing I would have you do is to decide on the one to three physical activities that you enjoy — walking, jogging, aerobics, biking, skating, skiing, rowing, swimming, jumping rope, playing basketball, or working out at a health club are only some of the many possibilities.

Determine to spend thirty minutes three times a week participating in any one of your selected activities (mix and match to your mood and energy level — it's also beneficial in working different muscles.) Okay, so you're *really* out of shape. Then start with five minutes and build up to five minutes five times each week. (These suggestions assume you have medical clearance from a physician.)

In your notebook keep track of the duration, date, and description of the activity. Sure, you may have setbacks. In fact, you probably will, so don't berate yourself when the time comes. What is important is that you make progress. On the other hand, beware of trying to make progress too rapidly. Pushing yourself too far beyond your norm may curtail rather than advance your ultimate progress.

Jeremy decided in mid-life that he had better do something to slow down the aging process, or at least try to keep from aging prematurely out of laziness and indifference.

He started by walking three evenings a week with his wife. At first he could hardly make it around the block without feeling his chest struggle for air. Rather than concentrating on a fixed time limit, Jeremy and his wife just walked until they were tired — no excruciating workouts, no injured muscles (sore maybe), no mental dreading of an unpleasant connection with self-imposed pain.

Jeremy and his wife looked forward to the companionship garnered from their evening promenades. They chatted with neighbors along the way and felt a sense of community. They seemed to have more vitality during the day; and they didn't drop into bed at night exhausted from a hectic, monotonous day.

All in all, Jeremy's life took a turn for the better when he decided to get out of his twenty-year slump. Today Jeremy and his wife intersperse their walks with horseback riding, sailing, and biking. Before, they didn't have the energy to enjoy pleasurable extras in their run-of-the-mill existence.

"Doesn't This Advice Get Any Better?"

The third area I would have you consider is diet. I recommend dealing with the exercise issue before diet because our appetite decreases if we maintain an exercise program. Also, the habits of self-discipline formed through exercise are valuable in developing new habits in other areas of our lives.

Books on health and diet abound. It is to our benefit to become knowledgeable about which foods are the most compatible with our bodies. *Greater Health God's Way,* on page 52, states: "Natural foods . . . promote strength, health, endurance, and life." A general rule that has been advocated far and wide is to eat food as close to its natural state as possible. That means we must develop a taste for raw fruits, vegetables, nuts, and foods made with whole grains. Become acquainted with the benefits of eating healthy foods simply. Feel the difference changing your diet can make in your life.

I have given up junk food for *real* food and have never regretted it. Well, maybe when I smell those fast food french fries, I think, *Can they really be all that bad?* Many of the foods I have eliminated from my diet may not be all that bad, but the reason I have eliminated them is because I know there is a better way to eat.

While in time management we must select the best of many good opportunities in which to invest our time, in our diet we need to select the foods that are the best nourishment for us.

A word of caution: when trying to change habits that took years to form, don't expect to have the same measure of discipline that took someone else many years to develop! I have a friend who has been trying to "fine-tune" her life this past year. She had made tremendous strides in developing self-discipline in every area. But instead of appreciating how much progress she has made over this past year, she sometimes compares her life to mine and gets discouraged. She needs to realize that I have been *working* at these principles for twelve years. She has made more headway last year than I ever did in any one year.

Compare yourself only with yourself based on who you are and who you can be in Jesus Christ. Be careful about patting yourself on the back just because you are above average. Are you the best *you* can be for *you,* not someone else?

Motivation for Change

Yes, developing discipline takes time and commitment. Just as we break our goals down into smaller, manageable segments, so too should we approach making changes in our lives, one step at a time.

But we must be certain in our minds *why* we want to improve in the first place. In the case of diet, it may be to lose weight so as to enhance our attractiveness, increase our stamina and energy, make it easier to breathe, live longer, or maybe just because we want to be faithful with the body that God has entrusted to us. Only then can we begin to tackle the segments.

Sandy had known for years that she should change her eating habits. She knew that she overate for emotional and psychological reasons, and she was aware that her whole life was being affected by her lack of discipline. But it wasn't until the doctor gave her an ultimatum, "Eat right, or die!" that she was jolted into reality. It finally sunk in that she had slowly poisoned herself. All right, now what? Sandy sought the help of a devoted friend and together they worked out a plan to help her turn her life around.

Sandy was so desperate that she wanted to go "cold turkey," but it would have shocked her system so badly that she decided on a three-stage plan instead.

Stage One: Eliminate desserts and substitute fresh fruits. This was a difficult assignment because Sandy had programmed herself to desire something sweet after every meal.

Stage Two: Replace refined cereals and breads with whole grain cereals and breads. Since our society has become cholesterol conscious in the last few years, products are plentiful that please your palate while picketing particularly poor passions. (Okay, so I like alliteration.)

Stage Three: Use jams made with fruit juice, do away with sugary drinks and sodas, substitute healthier snacks for potato chips. Sensible stuff. Sandy never went overboard for way-out foods with names she couldn't even pronounce, that looked as unappetizing as they sounded, and tasted even worse. But she did go back to the basics and learned to enjoy food in a new way.

It took many months to retrain her taste buds, and it wasn't all success. She experienced setbacks but refused to give in to the thinking, *Well, I've blown it. I might as well go buy a gallon of ice cream and wallow in my self-flagellation.*

One day Sandy was served a food that she hadn't eaten since the doctor's requiem. She was surprised to find the stronghold of its appeal almost nonexistent. She never would have believed it possible. She even found herself preferring healthy foods to the impostors of nutrition!

Along with changing your diet, I very strongly recommend taking supplements — all natural, highly researched, and tested. There are many books which explain the intricacies of natural versus synthetic vitamins. If you have no idea where to start and would like to know what line of products I recommend, write to me in care of this publisher.

The question always arises as to the need for supplements. Because our environment and food chain have been so altered in the last century we can no longer rely on getting optimum value from foods—even if we eat a purely natural diet. However, this is not meant to be a scientific spiel. I only know the amazing difference in my functioning as a human being when I take supplements regularly and when I don't. (Dave says AMEN!)

"I Could Never Do That!"

Fourth, I would encourage the practice of fasting one day a week. There are physical and spiritual benefits to fasting that cannot be denied. It would serve you well to read about them in more detail in one of the many books on the subject. Here it will suffice to tell you Donna's story.

Donna was normally an attractive brunette, now in her thirties. However, a car accident left her with a permanent injury, changing her life drastically. Her physical limitations ruled out the jogging that had been her recreation and standard exercise.

Donna had never had a problem with her weight because she was so active. But after two years of not being able to participate in strenuous activity, she began to put on some unsightly pounds. In fact, food itself went from the background to the foreground in her life.

She began to depend on it to supply what the injury took away. Feelings of self-pity manifested themselves in chocolate binges or potato chip frenzies. Her self-discipline began to crumble in every area. First it was the eating, then it was her temper. After that, it was the overspending, and finally, she allowed immorality to infiltrate her life.

Donna felt as if she was out of control, and despair threatened to overtake her at every turn. Some days she felt like banging her head against a wall to relieve the pressure she felt building, building, building. Other days she had so little energy that she dreaded the thought of pulling back the covers.

Then Donna read a book about the benefits of fasting—especially how fasting can help you gain control of your life. A spark of hope flickered in Donna that day. Maybe she could stop the downward spiral to total desperation.

Donna started by missing one meal the first week, increased it to two the next, and by the third week, she fasted a whole day. It was the longest day of her life. She felt sick to her stomach, weak, and dizzy. She almost gave up several times, even though she was drinking fruit juices to cleanse her system from the obvious build-up of toxins.

But she made it! She felt so victorious that night that she wanted to stay awake just to relish it. It was the best she felt *about* herself since the accident. As Donna fasted week after week, she noticed her craving of junk food decreased, her energy level increased, and most amazing of all, she began to regain self-control in the other areas of her life as well.

After a time, on her fasting day Donna began to focus on a specific area of need to bring before the Lord throughout the day. She stood in awe of the many direct answers to prayer. She cultivated her relationship with the Lord so much so that others began to notice the difference.

She was calmer and took more care of her personal appearance. Her family wasn't sure what was going on, but they liked the changes! The measure of discipline that Donna gained through fasting also served as a catalyst in leading her to purity.

Not only that, but Donna decided to do something positive about her lack of exercise. Sure, she was limited in what she could do. But at least she could start walking, albeit slowly. And she could move around in a pool or hot tub to work her muscles.

Interestingly, even the small efforts she made at exercise did wonders for her. She noticed an improvement in her stamina and ability to withstand the pain from her injury, a feeling of being refreshed and totally relaxed, a mental alertness, and a general sense of well-being that visited her more and more frequently.

"It's About Time You Started Talking My Language!"

All right, so we finally get to the one you have been waiting for: rest and relaxation. Rest is not an option if we are to function at our best, but sometimes we try to feed emotional needs by not allowing ourselves to rest. We may try to feel important by giving the impression that the world would fall apart if it didn't have our input. Or, we may keep spinning our wheels because we are afraid to face ourselves, our past, our future, our pain. Perhaps guilt motivates us to push, push, push. The guilt imposed by a spouse, parents, teachers, and a faulty concept of God leads us to think that we will be more worthy if we keep working.

There is a principle evident here similar to the tithe. Ninety percent of our income goes farther while tithing than 100 percent does while not tithing. So, too, does our expended energy. It goes farther with rest than it does without rest.

We need to give ourselves permission to let go and enjoy life. There is a place for seriousness, work, and pain. But there is also a place for fun, laughter, and pleasure. Life is made up of balances. Neglect any one area and your life is sure to suffer for it.

It takes discipline for some of us to allow ourselves to have a good time. We must retrain our thinking about the purpose of re-laxation. Even the almighty God rested the seventh day after com-pleting creation. Do you suppose it was to give us an example rather than because He needed to?

Times of play enhance our creativity and spontaneity, while work offers the fulfillment of a purpose. We need both work and play to truly enjoy life. Though our goal is to enjoy the Lord and glorify Him, we are told that Christ has "come that [we] may have life, and have it to the full" (John 10:10). Think about it. What does having life to the full mean to you? How does that picture differ from what you are experiencing right now? What has to change in order for you to have life to the full?

Ed is the kind of guy people envy. He has both depth of charac-ter and an obvious enjoyment of life. He laughs so heartily that care and worry just vanish. His delight in people and day-to-day events makes people want to savor every minute with him.

Ed's goal in life is to give people the freedom to laugh and have fun. His charisma and charm are outdone only by his sensitivity and love for others. He accomplishes as much or more than the next fellow, but he seems to have such a good time doing it! Would that all of us were able to have that kind of attitude about life!

An expanded discussion that ties together all these components of developing physical self-discipline is available in one very special volume. The absolute best book I have read over the years on the subject of health and nutrition (and I've read hundreds) is *Greater Health God's Way* by Stormie Omartian. It is one of those rare books that needs to be read on an annual basis.

"So, That's Why . . ."

I believe in taking advantage of cycles and moods as much as possible. Since I'm not a man, I can't testify to what they experience; but for women, life often revolves around cycles. Harmony in the family can rise and fall on cycles, especially if teen-aged girls are part of the home. It could make for nonending conflict if not recognized and dealt with as such.

The difference in estrogen levels in a woman's body during various times of the month correlates to a predictable pattern of behaviors and emotions. In general, during the first week of her cycle she is outgoing, ambitious, optimistic, self-disciplined, independent, and self-confident. During the second week she is hopeful, easygoing, creative, sensitive to beauty, peaceful, idealistic, tolerant, and has inner strength and a sense of well-being. At the time of ovulation she is content, accepting, romantic and sentimental, sexually assertive, patient, and somewhat passive.

The third week she lacks coordination, longs for peace, loses interest in life, moves slowly, is plagued by self-doubt, is impatient, apprehensive, moody, and gloomy. The fourth week she is very irritable, touchy, withdrawn, unreasonable, quarrelsome, impatient, moody, lazy, has food cravings and binges, is prone to unpredictable outbursts of emotion, and lacks self-confidence.

Whew! Is it any wonder that interpersonal conflicts sometimes seem to come from nowhere? Naturally, these characteristics are not true for all women, and some women struggle with them more than others (and their families struggle right along with them).

Maybe you need to tell yourself, "Tomorrow or next week will be better" or "It will soon pass, just hang in there!" Certain weeks simply are not ideal for making major decisions because they will often be poor ones. Make your plans during your better weeks, and allow the strength of positive habits to carry you through when it seems as if the end will never come.

There are some things you can do to alleviate the disastrous effects that premenstrual syndrome (PMS) brings with it:

Exercise regularly. Exercise helps to restore equilibrium during the stress of PMS.

Maintain an especially healthy diet. Because of the food cravings common to PMS, it is important to have developed good nutritional habits during the weeks when your self-discipline level is high.

Drink plenty of water. Pure water helps us to cut down on excess body fat, increase muscle tone, improve certain digestive problems, eliminate some toxins, alleviate some joint and muscle soreness, and guard against excessive water retention.

Other cycles influence our bodies as well. During certain times of the year we seem to have more energy along with the frame of mind to begin new projects (spring and fall are often the natural renewal times for many people). The same is true with regard to months, weeks, and days. Weather affects some individuals more than others. Work with your body, but don't be afraid to train it to do what you want it to do. Paul says in 1 Corinthians 9:27, "I beat my body and make it my slave so that after I have preached to others, I myself will not be disqualified for the prize."

Summary

Why bother developing physical self-discipline? Isn't life meant to be enjoyed? Because we are fearfully and wonderfully made (see Psalm 139:14) and our body is the temple of the Holy Spirit (see 1 Corinthians 3:16–17) and we are urged to give our bodies as a "living sacrifice" to the Lord (see Romans 12:1–2), then it is *very* important that we employ self-discipline in all matters related to the body.

Can you imagine living without the help of habits? Just suppose you had to concentrate on all the mundane things you do every day!

Your creative energies would be blocked, your conscious mind would be occupied with unimportant trivia, and you would have to overcome inertia in order to execute every motion.

One of the main challenges of life is to develop godly habits which free us to pursue that which is higher and more rewarding. There is a correlation between self-discipline and our ability to appreciate and enjoy God's blessings.

In order to change bad habits into good ones, try enacting the following steps:

- Identify the old or outdated habit (some habits outlive their usefulness). Since an inward desire must precede success, determine in your heart that you will pursue a change. Crisis often precipitates change and motivates us to redirect our course.
- Indicate in writing the new habit that you want to develop. You must know enough about the change you want to make in order to keep you from reverting to the old habit.
- Believe that with God's help you can replace the old with the new (see 2 Corinthians 5:17). Visualize yourself becoming the person that God wants you to be.
- Begin a new habit when outside stress is low. Begin strong and continue until it becomes a part of you.
- Take advantage of opportunities to put your new habit into practice. Our behavior is often a response to a stimulus. Pinpoint the reward that kept you practicing the old habit. Remove the reward, change the stimulus, or change your response to the stimulus. Reinforce your new behavior with a reward.

If you are having trouble, consider what promises you are capable of keeping and hold yourself to them (one day without desserts). At what point do you stop enjoying your habit and continue out of compulsion — one candy bar or three?

Build on your success. Stretch yourself. You made it today. See if you can go one more day. If we have self-discipline, we will respond to God's desire despite our emotions and appetites. We will live in harmony with the Word of God. We will follow the impulses of the Holy Spirit, not those of our flesh.

Chapter Challenge

Begin with the first challenge and work for thirty minutes. If you finish sooner, continue with the other challenges. Pick up the next day where you left off and spend thirty minutes proceeding through the list until each item has been completed.

1. Make a commitment in your heart to develop physical self-discipline. Don't worry about potential failures or setbacks. Everybody has them and they will surely come to you as well.

2. Begin by getting up one-half hour earlier once or twice a week and proceed from there. Monitor your rising times.

3. Choose two physical activities that you enjoy and begin an exercise program as mentioned in the chapter.

4. Set up a plan for changing to a healthier diet. Break it into manageable steps and implement the first one this week.

5. Skip one meal this week, two in one day next week, and fast a whole day the third week (provided you do not have any medical problems that would hinder you). Unsweetened juice fasting is often preferable to water fasting.

6. Determine if you are getting enough rest and relaxation. If not, plan once or twice a week for the next month, a special fun or restful time.

7. How can you better work with your body's natural energy levels? (Perform difficult tasks that need your concentration when you are the freshest; take a nap before the hectic hours of the day; reserve your light reading for your low energy times.)

8. Buy a copy of *Greater Health God's Way* by Stormie Omartian (Sparrow Press, 1984).

FIVE

DEVELOPING MENTAL SELF-DISCIPLINE

I t all began with a sales seminar across town. Carla had been as-
signed to the same small group as Shane. She had seen Shane
occasionally when he had passed through her department. It was a
large company, and Shane was responsible for product marketing
while she was part of the direct sales team.

During the small group discussion, Carla began to see Shane in
a different light. Where once he was just another management executive, now he seemed to be a lively personality. Where before he
was just another face in the sea of faces at the office, now he took on
an individuality that became less elusive. Where previously Shane
was known for his results, now he revealed the intelligence behind
those results.

Carla was fascinated by Shane's comments and input into the
discussion. He handled himself well, smiled purposefully, and had a
sensitivity lacking in most men. Carla felt more vibrant in response
to the colorful atmosphere Shane was painting. But all too soon it
was time to return to the larger group. *I haven't felt that alive in years!
Shane sure is something!* Carla thought to herself.

At lunchtime, Carla was one of the first through the buffet line.
A few minutes later, Shane made his way to Carla's table. He in

turn had been impressed with Carla's personality, her depth of insight, and her quiet beauty. She was confident and warm at the same time.

Lunch proved highly satisfying for Carla and Shane. Although both had spouses, they seemed to enjoy an ingredient today that was missing in their marriages. Their mutual attraction bordered on excitement, even though caution flags waved in their minds.

Their minds at this point could lead them to destruction or to character control. Maybe they wouldn't make a deliberate, conscious choice, but they would make a choice by default, nonetheless. For from that day Shane began to stop by Carla's office to chat more often. From time to time they would have what they called business lunches together to compare product notes. All the while, each replayed their brief encounters over and over in their minds.

What if he would ask me to dinner sometime?

I wonder if she would go for a drive with me some afternoon?

Does he really think I'm special?

She sure makes me feel like a man!

What if he were to . . . ?

What if she would . . . ?

Then the secret communication began. It seemed innocent enough. Shane would call either her office or home to ask how a new product package fared among the competition. But they would usually end up extending the conversation to talk about more personal things. Memos that began on a business tone would end on a personal one.

With each phone call and each note, it became easier to express thoughts that dominated their emotions. At each stage of the relationship, mental replay had first given permission for the chain of events to occur. No, things didn't always happen as Carla and Shane had fantasized, but they were ready to snatch any opportunity to deepen their friendship. Their eventual affair had been built scene by scene in their minds.

If you had asked Carla and Shane six months earlier if they would ever have an affair, each would have been aghast at the mere mention of it. They had solid Christian marriages and didn't seem to have any overt needs that weren't being fulfilled. Why, then, did their relationship end in an affair, ruining both marriages? Feasting mentally on the pleasures of being in one another's company brought with it the desire for repeated rendezvous.

Consciously and sometimes not so consciously, Carla and Shane arranged their day and their activities to allow for increased "chance" meetings to take place. They reached out to grasp the excitement of the moment. Their minds dwelled on their needs being met by each other. They had already given themselves permission in their minds long before their first night together.

Our actions, attitudes, habits, and character originate in the mind. Romans 12:1-2 tells us to be transformed by the renewing of our minds. Our minds, therefore, must have tremendous influence on what we become. True, the heart is deceitful and desperately wicked (Jeremiah 17:9). But, once we have been born again by the Spirit of God, we are new creatures (2 Corinthians 5:17) and are able to have the mind of Christ in us (Philippians 2:5).

Developing Mental Discipline

Here are some steps you can take to control your thinking so that it will be pleasing to God.

Read and memorize God's Word. I cannot overstate the importance of ingesting Scripture. Christ has already provided for our victory and has promised us the needed strength. In the book of Philippians Paul writes, "For it is God who works in you to will and to act according to his good purpose" (Philippians 2:13). God prompts us to look into His Word. We must then respond. By concentrating on God's thoughts, we build renewed strength to resist sinful thinking.

> Those who live according to the sinful nature have their minds set on what that nature desires; but those who live in accordance with the Spirit have their minds set on what the Spirit desires. The mind of sinful man is death, but the mind controlled by the Spirit is life and peace; the sinful mind is hostile to God. It does not submit to God's law, nor can it do so. Those controlled by the sinful nature cannot please God.

You, however, are controlled not by the sinful nature, but by the Spirit, if the Spirit of God lives in you. And if anyone does not have the Spirit of Christ, he does not belong to Christ. But if Christ is in you, your body is dead because of sin, yet your spirit is alive because of righteousness. And if the Spirit of him who raised Jesus from the dead is living in you, he who raised Christ from the dead will also give life to your mortal bodies through his Spirit, who lives in you. (Romans 8:5–11)

These verses describe two mindsets. Which controls your life? Amanda's husband, Nick, had a job which required an hour-long commute, both morning and evening. One day Nick bought a set of Scripture tapes to listen to while commuting. After several weeks Amanda began to notice subtle changes in Nick's character. For one thing, Nick's manner with the children was more gentle than before. And he was kind to that neighbor who always got on his nerves. He also chose television programs and radio stations more carefully. But what Amanda noticed most was his confidence in leading their family according to godly principles. Amanda had always felt the need to take the lead, because Nick usually just stayed in the background. What an impact Scripture was making on Nick and his world!

Focus on visual affirmations of what God wants you to be. By personalizing Scripture, we can feel its impact more powerfully. For example, substitute your name in John 3:16: "For God so loved _____ that he gave his one and only Son, that if _____ believes in him _____ shall not perish but have eternal life."

Or Psalm 1:2, "But *my* delight is in the law of the Lord, and on *Your* law *I* meditate day and night."

We control our behavioral patterns by what we tell ourselves. Now, what we tell ourselves may not always be the truth; however, we tend to act on what we *believe* to be true. This is where self-talk comes in. We can change our lives by the mental tapes we play over and over. Philippians exhorts us, "Whatever is true, whatever is noble, whatever is right, whatever is pure, whatever is lovely, whatever is admirable — if anything is excellent or praiseworthy — think about such things" (Philippians 4:8).

If we are faithful to apply this principle, then we will not have time to develop negative and destructive thought patterns. Our thoughts affect our emotions, and our emotions affect our behavior.

We need to line up our thinking with Scripture and replace untruth with God's truth. Otherwise we may fall into the trap of replacing one lie with another. Become conscious of the mental tapes you play to yourself.

Jason's self-image was destroyed by the time he was five. His parents and relatives labeled Jason a loser. Jason was awkward, he stuttered, and he had big ears and a funny nose. The more his family harped about his inadequacies, the more self-conscious he became.

As a teen-ager Jason developed his athletic prowess, and his head caught up with his ears in size. He had learned to apply himself in school and even made the National Honor Society. But no matter how well Jason did in school or how handsome he was becoming or how many athletic awards he won, he still felt second-rate. He couldn't shake the feeling of inadequacy. His mental picture of himself seemed incongruous with the good things his teachers and friends were telling him.

What Jason needs to do is to line up his thinking about himself with what God says about him. If he did, he would learn that Christ's death was a statement of Jason's value in God's eyes (1 Peter 1:18-19). He would learn that God accepts him unconditionally (Ephesians 2:8-9). And Jason would learn that he can become a new creature through Jesus Christ (2 Corinthians 5:17). When Jason fully realizes these truths, he will have the freedom to accept himself and become what God has intended for him to become — without the bondage of self-lies.

We all need to isolate our hangups, look into the Scriptures to see what God has to say about them, and then replace our self-lies with God's truth.

Allow for accountability in your life. By making yourself accountable to someone, whether to a friend, an older person you respect, or perhaps a relative, your success in developing mental self-discipline will increase greatly. Not only will you receive positive feedback, but being accountable will also motivate you to stay on the right track. When you do stray, you will receive the gift of another's firm love.

Barry knew he had a problem with money. His parents had always given him what he wanted — the latest electronic toys, a three-wheeler, and even the first car he wanted. He took ski vacations, cruises, and week-long trail rides in the mountains. His parents provided for his college education and gave him plenty of spending money. When he graduated they even gave him a nest-egg of fifty thousand dollars! He had lost a lot of that gambling, but he was sure he could win it back if he just tried a little harder.

Barry had a good-paying job — one he enjoyed well enough. But his thoughts dwelled on money, money, money. To his credit, he sincerely wanted to be free from money's dominance in his life.

Gordon grew up with Barry, but they had gone their separate ways. Now, many years later, Gordon was leasing an apartment in the same complex as Barry. After a grand reunion, weeks of normal routine, and several intense discussions, Barry told Gordon about his preoccupation with money. Gordon agreed to help Barry conquer the battle that constantly raged within him. Together they decided on a plan of attack for which Gordon would hold Barry accountable. No, Barry wasn't free overnight, but by the consistent love and determination of a friend, Barry started to gain control over his weakness.

Identify your blind spots and comfort zones. A blind spot is a weak area in our life of which we are unaware. This weak area could hinder us in several ways: it may keep us from personal growth, it may be a barrier between us and someone else, or it may affect how we feel about God.

By allowing God to reveal our blind spots to us, usually through someone else, we can begin to work though those areas and gain a measure of control over them. As we eliminate our blind spots, we will be able to focus mentally to a much greater degree on becoming Christlike. But avoidance tactics, either conscious or subconscious, will weaken our mental energy and perhaps even render us ineffective in the important issues of life.

In junior high Trisha picked up the habit of rolling her eyeballs whenever she thought something was stupid, or when she didn't want to do what her instructors or her parents told her. Although Trisha never outgrew this habit, she didn't realize that she still practiced it. That is, until one irritated co-worker pointed it out to her. By that time she had already alienated several would-be friends and had lost some possible promotions — all because of a negative, outdated habit.

With this new information Trisha could choose either to retaliate against her co-worker or to be mature and do something constructive about her habit. She chose to do something about it. As a result of gaining control in this area, Trisha was able to focus her mental energies on growing in other areas as well.

Our comfort zones involve that which is familiar. The familiar may be pleasant or unpleasant, but it is comfortable for us. Joey was raised in a low-income housing project and knew nothing else growing up. He was comfortable with his group of friends, although the world looked on in pity.

Joey was good in basketball — good enough to make the first string in high school. He had a style on the court that made the crowds go wild with excitement. In his senior year a basketball scout noticed him, and after graduation Joey was swept away to play for a select school, and then went on to the pros.

But Joey was never really comfortable associating with the upper class circles in which he found himself. Even though some would say it's not possible, Joey felt more comfortable in the housing project where he grew up than he did in the fancy hotels and restaurants he frequented as a basketball celebrity.

Comfort zones sometimes inhibit us; other times they spur us on to new heights of growth. It all depends on how we approach them. If our whole purpose in life is to keep safely within the boundaries of our comfort areas, then we will stifle opportunities for growth. By identifying our comfort zones, we can determine if we are refusing an opportunity for growth because God really does not want us to pursue it or simply because it goes beyond our own comfortable limits.

By focusing on what God says and not on our own comfort, we can expand in ways we never thought possible — through acceptance, endurance, frustration, and even pain. This brings us back to what God has been telling us all along:

"Therefore, prepare your minds for action; be self-controlled" (1 Peter 1:13).

"You were taught . . . to be made new in the attitude of your minds" (Ephesians 4:23).

"Set your minds on things above, not on earthly things" (Colossians 3:2).

"We take captive every thought to make it obedient to Christ" (2 Corinthians 10:5).

"You will keep in perfect peace him whose mind is steadfast because he trusts in you" (Isaiah 26:3).

And finally, "For God did not give us a spirit of timidity, but a spirit of power, of love and of self-discipline" (2 Timothy 1:7).

Summary

As a man thinks, so is he (see Proverbs 23:7). As we contemplate and meditate on spiritual truths, we allow the Spirit of God to transform us into the likeness of Jesus Christ.

Temptation tests our commitment and loyalty, develops our spiritual maturity and sensitivity, and gives opportunity to exhibit God's grace and power (see Romans 5:20). Our response to temptation is often a measure of our love for God.

Discipline your thinking by following these steps:

Read and memorize God's Word. Read the words, picture and experience the image, feel the emotion.

Focus on affirming what God wants you to be. Personalize Scripture by putting it in the present tense and relating it to your life.

Allow for accountability in your life. Willingly become answerable to a friend or respected leader for your actions.

Identify your blind spots and comfort zones, and then determine to make any necessary changes.

Chapter Challenge

Begin with the first challenge and work for thirty minutes. If you finish sooner, continue with the other challenges. Pick up the next day where you left off and spend thirty minutes proceeding through the list until each item has been completed.

1. Ask the Holy Spirit to make you aware of the areas in which you have an undisciplined mind.

2. Why would it be harmful for you to continue this line of thinking in each of these areas? What would be the benefits of bringing these thoughts under the subjection of Jesus Christ? (2 Corinthians 10:3-5).

3. Select one area where your mind needs to be renewed so that you may be transformed. Look up Scripture passages that relate directly to this area. Memorize three of the verses.

4. Develop a plan for combating undisciplined thinking in this area. For example: Suppose you wanted control over thinking negative thoughts. Your plan of attack might be:

   a. Ask the Holy Spirit to make you aware each time you have a negative thought.

   b. Look up and memorize three to five verses on having the mind of Christ.

   c. Each time you think a negative thought, replace it with one of the verses you memorized.

   d. Ask a friend to point out when your negative thinking affects your speech or attitudes.

   e. Praise God for His faithfulness in transforming you by His power.

   f. Repeat Scripture verses to yourself as you fall off to sleep.

5. Describe a day or an hour when you were on top of the world and your mental well-being was at its best. Why do you think it was so? How can you re-create it?

6. Ask the Lord to point out any blind spots or comfort zones that are inhibiting your growth.

DEVELOPING EMOTIONAL SELF-DISCIPLINE

E motions. Can you imagine a life without them? Sure, it may be easier, it may be less complicated, and it may be more efficient. But how dull, how colorless, how unexciting! Emotions are a gift from God. To refuse to recognize them severs us from living with the fullness that can be ours through Jesus Christ.

One day Andrew decided that he had had enough. His emotions spelled trouble whenever he let them out of their cage. They had caused him so much grief and frustration that he just decided to live his life without them. From then on he refused to get angry, avoided caring about anyone, and ignored his conscience. Yes, he was sure this was going to be a better way to live!

As the months passed into years, friends began falling away one by one. That was okay, because Andrew didn't care anyway. He just continued to exist in his own world. Even when his wife left with the children, Andrew ignored the pangs that threatened to surface.

At ball games when his team won the championship, Andrew took a ho-hum attitude and wouldn't let himself celebrate with the rest of his team. He was thinking about quitting anyway. Hitting a little ball around seemed infantile to him now. Andrew spent more and more time by himself, and life became meaningless and boring. True, he did not struggle with emotions any more, but neither did he seem to enjoy life the way he used to. Oh, well, he had made his decision and he wasn't going to turn back now. He wished life would hurry up and get over. . . .

Gaining self-discipline over our emotions does not mean repressing or ignoring them. Our emotions can be strong allies if we recognize them, work through what they mean to us, and then choose to act a certain way to bring about positive and healthy changes in our lives. Our negative emotions may be signaling us to pay attention to inner wounds which need God's healing grace. And when we fear our negative emotions and refuse to accept them, we limit our ability to appreciate positive emotions as well. Sure, we may barricade ourselves in our narrow comfort zone, but if we do, we will miss many blessings along the way.

Brief Description of Major Emotions

This is not meant to be a volume on the psychology of emotions, but rather a highlighting of various emotions, how they affect us, and how we can better control them so as to live happier lives. A general plan for gaining emotional control at the end of this chapter outlines many steps which apply to gaining control over any emotion.

Anxiety

Anxiety, or worry, (for our purpose we will refer to them interchangeably) often involves concern about a future happening based on our view of present circumstances.

Kay was a leading executive in a prestigious company. It had not been easy on the long climb to her current position. In fact, if you could follow her trail of anxiety you would find that her worries negated any happiness her accomplishments might have brought her.

She was a nervous wreck for an entire week before the first interview. She couldn't eat right, got little sleep, and was super touchy at home. But she had handled it well enough. During the breaking-in period, she was constantly fighting an acid stomach.

Was she catching on quickly enough to the new company's policies and procedures?

After that came the anxiety over whether her peers were accepting her. She found herself eavesdropping on conversations, replaying daily events in her mind, and trying to determine hidden meanings in what people said to her. And now she was in a state of dread over an upcoming performance review. How would she measure up? What if she were dismissed? What if they thought she should be producing more results? What if . . . ?

Anxiety touches most of us at some time in our lives because we are human. But we can choose to succumb to its clutches, suffocating our joy, or we can do something positive to bring it under submission.

Anxiety affects people of all ages. Pre-schoolers may experience sickening fear when they are left in an unfamiliar environment or walk by the neighbor's dog. Elementary children may fear an antagonistic teacher or big bully down the street. Junior highers may fear not making the cheerleading squad or basketball team. High schoolers may fear not having a date or not being in the popular crowd.

Anxiety may come to college students in the form of semester exams or coming to terms with the realities of life. The awesome responsibility of raising two small children or the thought of her husband having an affair may paralyze a young mother. For the middle-aged man, it may be the disappointment of unrealized dreams or the weight of meeting financial obligations. For the older woman, it may be coming to terms with the empty nest or acknowledging her deteriorating and aging body. And, for the elderly, it may be trying to cope with loneliness and helplessness or fear of life after death.

Whatever our situation, the underlying causes of much of our anxiety stem from outside pressures which strangle our sense of control. Unmet expectations of ourselves and others further undermine our well-being.

Anxiety is that sick, strange feeling in your chest or the pit of your stomach that signals unrest, that screams, "All is not well!" It's not a fun way to live, but sometimes we feel powerless to change our course. Sometimes we feel helpless to command anxiety, "Be gone!"; sometimes we feel like a prisoner of our own sentencing, and the key to our self-made cage has been thrown away.

But there is hope. Scripture gives us the assurance that peace can be ours through Jesus Christ.

"Peace I leave with you; my peace I give you. I do not give to you as the world gives. Do not let your hearts be troubled and do not be afraid" (John 14:27).

"The mind of sinful man is death, but the mind controlled by the Spirit is life and peace" (Romans 8:6).

"For he [Jesus Christ] himself is our peace" (Ephesians 2:14).

"Do not be anxious about anything, but in everything, by prayer and petition, with thanksgiving, present your requests to God. And the peace of God, which transcends all understanding, will guard your hearts and your minds in Christ Jesus" (Philippians 4:6-7).

Fear

I remember a recurring nightmare I had as a child in which I had gotten up to go to the bathroom. When I reached my bedroom door, it was closed and locked. I kept trying to pull at the door handle but it wouldn't budge. Then I started banging on the door with my fists. In the dark room frustration and fear mounted as I pounded on the door and screamed and cried for someone to let me out. Trying to ignore my full bladder, I concentrated all my efforts on escape. That's all I remember.

But my mother tells me that she and my dad would hear me screaming and come upstairs to find me sleepwalking again. Then they would pull me off of the windows at the opposite end of the room from the door. In my sleep I would climb up on a window seat, thinking it was the door. Many years later my mother expressed their concern that on summer nights the window would be open and I might fall to my death on the sidewalk below.

Fear incapacitates and paralyzes us. Past experiences can haunt us even as adults, even though they left our conscious minds long ago. Fear numbs and stagnates. Although certain temperaments are more prone to fear, we all have occasions when fear is very real in our lives.

Not all fear is debilitating. In fact, some is healthy. It causes us to limit our activities for fear of the repercussions. It protects us from possible danger. It motivates us to change.

Lindsey was afraid of meeting new people. When she was small her family had moved a lot, and she was always an outsider. Just when she would overcome her fear of getting to know the kids, her family would move again. But the fear seemed to get bigger and bigger with each move.

Then one day, Lindsey just decided not to try any more. She closed a part of herself off and made no attempt to get to know anyone. She built a wall of stone around her heart. No more would she have to face rejection or loneliness. No more would she weep at friends left behind. No more would she regret all that could not be. She became an island unto herself. By now Lindsey was in high school and didn't have one friend. She was cold and empty inside.

How tragic that Lindsey's fears, although real and perhaps justified, would cripple her for the rest of her life. We all have obstacles to overcome in our lives, whether it be certain fears, a physical handicap, or a volatile home situation. It is never easy to conquer obstacles or to go forward, perhaps an inch at a time. It is not easy to deal with setbacks that in themselves are worse than the original circumstances.

But through Jesus Christ we can master our fears. There is hope for even the most fearful:

"There is no fear in love. But perfect love drives out fear, because fear has to do with punishment. The one who fears is not made perfect in love" (1 John 4:18).

"So do not fear, for I am with you; do not be dismayed, for I am your God. I will strengthen you and help you; I will uphold you with my righteous right hand" (Isaiah 41:10).

He who dwells in the shelter of the Most High will rest in the shadow of the Almighty. I will say of the Lord, "He is my refuge and my fortress, my God, in whom I trust." Surely he will save you from the fowler's snare and from the deadly pestilence. He will cover you with his feathers, and under his wings you will find refuge; his faithfulness will be your shield and rampart. You will not fear the terror of night, nor the arrow that flies by day, nor the pestilence that stalks in the darkness, nor the plague that destroys at midday. A thousand may fall at your side, ten thousand at your right hand, but it will not come near you. You will only observe with your eyes and see the punishment of the wicked. If you make the Most High your dwelling—even the Lord, who is my refuge—then no harm will befall you, no disaster will come near your tent. For he will command his angels concerning you to guard you in all your ways. (Psalm 91:1–11)

Hate/Resentment

As a child, Deborah was abused by her father. For many years she dwelled on the revenge she would someday inflict on him. Deborah plotted retaliation in her heart until it consumed her. Her hatred for her father colored all her other relationships.

Friends sensed her bitterness and resentment. Though Deborah was a beautiful girl, the hatred in her heart repelled any would-be suitors. Ugliness reared up in many forms that seemed unrelated to her father.

Deborah could slice someone to the core with her venomous tongue and hateful words that spewed in every direction. She could use sarcasm and haughty talk until it made her opponents slink away in defeat. Deborah vowed that she wouldn't let her father get the best of her, but he was doing just that by enslaving her in memories that cried out for revenge.

We often think we will get even for a wrong committed against us. My mother used to tell me when I would harbor resentment in my heart that I was only hurting myself. I know what she meant. By allowing bitterness to fester, we chain ourselves to a way of life that is neither abundant nor enjoyable. Beyond that, Scripture commands us to deal with our bitterness and hatred and allow it to have no part in our lives.

"We love because he first loved us. If anyone says, 'I love God,' yet hates his brother, he is a liar. For anyone who does not love his brother, whom he has seen, cannot love God, whom he has not seen. And he has given us this command: Whoever loves God must also love his brother" (1 John 4:19–21).

"Anyone who claims to be in the light but hates his brother is still in the darkness. Whoever loves his brother lives in the light, and there is nothing in him to make him stumble. But whoever hates his brother is in the darkness and walks around in the darkness; he does not know where he is going, because the darkness has blinded him" (1 John 2:9–11).

Jealousy/Envy

Marty had always been number one in high school. Number one on the football team, number one with the girls, number one in academics, number one as his parents' only child. He was used to being doted upon and getting anything he wanted.

Marty had expected life always to be so — with the world bowing to his every wish. He pitied the poor souls who seemed spellbound to serve him. But his pity was short-lived. Arriving on his college campus in a neighboring state, Marty realized for the first time that the world was *not* at his beck and call. As one in a sea of fifty thousand students, Marty suddenly had no social prestige. He was an unknown.

Before long he had singled out the select few who were where he *should* be. He envied their position as BMOC's (Big Men On Campus) and lusted for similar status. He was jealous of their achievements, judgmental of their adulation, and jeered at their abilities. Marty was miserable. Envy kept him from forming meaningful friendships because he thought he deserved better. Sulking and seething became his way of life.

We cause our own demise when we nurse envy and jealousy in our hearts. Whether it be for another's wife, house, or career, we gain nothing by allowing jealousy to infiltrate our lives. On the contrary, we deprive ourselves of the freedom to be content in who we are and what we have.

A child's mother buys her a new dress, perhaps denying herself a much-needed pair of shoes. Her daughter is overwhelmed with gratitude and proudly models the dress for all the family to see. At church the next day she prances in front of all her friends; that is, until she meets the daughter of a wealthy visitor. The once grateful child now compares her nice dress to the visitor's stunning one. All of a sudden, the dress that brought such joy to the child yesterday doesn't seem special anymore. She allowed envy to rob her of something very precious.

Scripture admonishes us, "[Love] does not envy" (1 Corinthians 13:4) and "Above all, love each other deeply, because love covers over a multitude of sins" (1 Peter 4:8). Love, then, seems to be the antidote for jealousy and envy. We will give more specific steps to conquer these upsetting emotions at the end of the chapter.

Unresolved Anger

Terry could feel the heated emotions overtaking him — again. If his wife made one more derogatory comment about his father, he would have to resort to drastic measures to get her attention.

Terry's wife and his father seemed locked in a personality conflict. True, *her* father may be more loving, less sarcastic, and less controlling, but that was no reason for her to hurl insults at him and his father. Why, she even accused him of acting just like his father! He did not, and just to show her, he was going to demonstrate what it really meant to be controlling. . . .

Anger often brings with it the desire for retaliation. It screams for immediate action — either to douse it or to fan it. We may repress it, refusing to acknowledge the anger that threatens our control. Or we may allow it to fester and infect us to the point of irrational behavior.

James admonishes us, "My dear brothers, take note of this: Everyone should be quick to listen, slow to speak and slow to become angry, for man's anger does not bring about the righteous life that God desires. Therefore, get rid of all moral filth and the evil that is so prevalent and humbly accept the word planted in you, which can save you" (James 1:19–21).

We may find ourselves getting angry over unmet expectations, feelings of helplessness, or insignificant irritations. Josh's pre-conceived ideas of family behavior came from "Leave it to Beaver" and "Father Knows Best." So his thirteen-year-old daughter's blossoming independence exasperated him a great deal. Carol Anne's precise ideas about how she should live her life — her manner of dressing, her language, and her friends — fueled a growing torrent of rage in Josh.

Now, to be fair, Carol Anne's clothes were modest, but they were not the feminine dresses Josh wanted her to wear. Her language was not obscene, just "in." And her friends were not wild, just different from the preppie types Josh thought his daughter should befriend. Here we have a case of anger caused by unmet expectations. Did Josh have a right to those expectations? Did he have a right to his anger?

On the other hand, Carol Anne was also becoming increasingly angry. She felt helpless to control her situation. Her dad was bigger than she was, could withhold her allowance, and in general could make life miserable if she did not conform to his wishes. But to do so made Carol Anne feel as if she were betraying her personhood. This inner conflict increased the anger and screamed for a resolution.

After a crescendo of crises one weekend, Josh and Carol Anne agreed that they needed to take some positive action. By working through this situation with lots of give and take on both parts, Josh and Carol Anne were able to reach a solution that dissipated the continuing anger in each of them.

Josh allowed Carol Anne more freedom to choose her friends and clothes. Carol Anne would refrain from using her "in" language at home, make an effort to acquaint her friends and parents, and agree to not buy or wear something that particularly irritated her father.

In itself anger may not be wrong. Anger over greed and disrespect motivated Jesus to overturn the money changers' tables in the temple area (see Matthew 21:12–13). Anger over injustice motivated Martin Luther King, Jr., to fight for his dream and in so doing change the course of American history.

And anger over the trampling of family values spurred Beverly LaHaye to form Concerned Women of America — an organization whose voice is moving legal mountains in favor of traditional family values across the country.

Pride

Pride is probably the most subtle of the emotions. We can be infected with the disease of pride and not even feel sick. Trudy was extremely prideful. But, though others could see it, Trudy was blind to its invasion of her personal relationships.

At social gatherings, Trudy pretended a superior knowledge that everyone else knew she didn't possess. She constantly belittled others while elevating herself. Trudy's haughty spirit warned others not to cross her. In short, Trudy had succumbed to the sin of pride, and people downright didn't like her because of it.

Pride may stem from a superiority complex, or its opposite, an inferiority complex. Most of us are guilty of one or the other at some point in our lives. We will have victory over the sin of pride to the degree that we allow the Spirit of God to transform us. We can even be proud of thinking we are not proud!

Now pride has its proper place. Being proud of a job well done or proud of our children is the positive facet of this emotion, just as each of the emotions have positive aspects to them.

The opposite of pride is humility. One of the best ways to develop humility is to serve others. Serving others does not have to be akin to slave labor; it can be doing something we enjoy that benefits someone else. Perhaps you are a carpenter. You could do some odd jobs for a widow in your church. Maybe you like to sew. You could do some mending for the elderly gentleman in your neighborhood. Or, you may enjoy gardening. You could give your homegrown vegetables to a few shut-ins. Serving should be an extension of ourselves, our gifts, and our hearts.

God's Word commands us to be humble: "Clothe yourselves with humility toward one another, because, 'God opposes the proud but gives grace to the humble.' Humble yourselves, therefore, under God's mighty hand, that he may lift you up in due time" (1 Peter 5:5–6).

"Therefore, as God's chosen people, holy and dearly loved, clothe yourselves with compassion, kindness, humility, gentleness and patience. Bear with each other and forgive whatever grievances you may have against one another" (Colossians 3:12–13).

"Do nothing out of selfish ambition or vain conceit, but in humility consider others better than yourselves" (Philippians 2:3).

Positive Emotions

What about the positive emotions—do we need to control them too? Isn't it good just to let them flow? In the brief discussion that follows, we will not dissect each emotion but rather mention how discipline relates to each one.

So much has been written about the need for love, joy, peace, excitement for living, caring, and contentment. True, some of these can be classified as heart attitudes. But they each also generate specific emotions.

We need discipline to *love,* or show love at the proper times, which in itself is often a measure of love. Neal had a genuine love for people. He bent over backwards to help them whenever he could —even when the recipient would have learned a greater lesson doing it himself. Neal showered gifts on ladies in the neighborhood until they thought he had ulterior motives. He tried so hard to help people that he often became a nuisance and people resented his help! What do you think? Should Neal have used more discipline, more discretion, in working out his love?

Our expressions of *excitement* may be out of line. Jennifer, a bubbly-type person, loved to show her excitement. But sometimes it embarrassed those around her, and they took it for a sign of immaturity. Sometimes Jennifer displayed her excitement at inappropriate occasions, like the time she received a dozen roses from her boyfriend on the same day as her co-worker's tenth wedding anniversary—forgotten again this year. Or when she excitedly modeled a new dress for her parents when she knew they could not even pay their overdue electric bill.

Contentment carried to the extreme ends in apathy—lacking concern for anything. We are to be involved in caring. We can't just sit back under the guise of being content with things as they are. If they can be changed to better reflect the characteristics of Jesus Christ, then it is our responsibility to act toward that end.

Peace does not always mean inaction or noninvolvement. It would be more peaceful to give in to a wailing five-year-old. It would be more peaceful to watch the world go by as legislation is passed that destroys Christian values. It would be more peaceful to let those suffering under a tyrannical political system fend for themselves. No, peace at any cost is not the issue. Some things are worth fighting for. It takes discipline to move ourselves toward a greater peace than perhaps immediate circumstances warrant.

We need a measure of discipline filtered through the positive emotions to bring balance to our Christian lives. It becomes an individual matter. What is right for me may not be right for you. What you feel God would have you do may be different from what He wants me to do in the same situation, provided neither of us violates the absolutes of Scripture.

Gaining Emotional Control

It is to this end that we have been directing our course. Whether it be gaining control of our anxiety, fear, hatred, jealousy, anger, or pride, Scripture promises and exhortations offer hope for change.

Part 1—Inward Decision

- Initiate steps toward gaining control. We can't wait for someone else to take action when we are the ones that need to change (Philippians 3:13-14).
- Indicate your desire before the Lord to become all that He wants you to be (Colossians 2:6-7).
- Inquire of the Lord what it is He would have you do about the emotional areas of your life (Matthew 7:7-8).
- Incline your ear to the Lord and listen to His voice (Luke 10:39).
- Identify the areas where you need to change (James 1:5).
- Investigate what God's Word says about the change (2 Timothy 3:16).
- Isolate instances where you need to ask forgiveness (Colossians 3:13).
- Itemize the things you need to do to make restitution (Proverbs 6:31).
- Intoxicate yourself with the Holy Spirit, bring your life under His influence and control (Ephesians 5:18).
- Imagine ways that God could use you (Ephesians 1:11-12).

Part 2—Indicators of Inward Decision

- Intend to change with God's help (2 Corinthians 5:16-17).
- Immerse yourself in Scripture (Psalm 1:2).
- Individualize and personalize Scripture (Psalm 119:11).

- Install these principles in your life (Colossians 3:7-10).
- Infiltrate Scripture into your thinking (Romans 12:1-2).
- Invalidate self-lies — things you learned in childhood that do not match up with what God says about you (Psalm 139:13-16; 1 Peter 1:18-19).
- Interfere with your old line of thought and exchange it for a new way of thinking according to God's Word (Philippians 4:8).
- Invade your old repertoire of habits (Colossians 3:5-10).
- Inflate Jesus Christ's position in your life (John 3:30).

Part 3 — Interchange in Growth

- Impress God's Word upon your heart (2 Timothy 3:14-17).
- Inflame your passion for righteousness (Matthew 6:33).
- Impair Satan's attacks by resisting him (James 4:7).
- Insulate yourself from defeat by putting on the whole armor of God (Ephesians 6:10-18).

Part 4 — Impact on the World

- Introduce others to Jesus Christ (Acts 1:8) and invite others to accept Him as Lord of their lives (John 3:16).
- Interest others with the things of God (2 Corinthians 5:18-21).
- Include others in your ministry (1 Corinthians 12:27).
- Involve others in using their gifts (1 Corinthians 12).
- Interact with others through accountability (1 Corinthians 4:1-2).
- Inform others about the things of God (Colossians 2:2-4).
- Instruct others about the ways of the Lord (Philippians 2:1-4).
- Impart lessons to others through your example (Titus 2:7-8).
- Intrigue others with the wonders of God (Psalm 105).
- Influence others for the glory of God (2 Corinthians 2:14-17).
- Invest in the lives of others (Colossians 1:28-29).
- Inspire others toward godliness (1 Timothy 2:2).

IMPLEMENT THESE STEPS!

Summary

God has created us as emotional beings. In working toward emotional health it is helpful if we admit our feelings and acknowledge our needs, request the support of friends, realize that blessing follows obedience, and give thanks in spite of emotional struggle.

The more we can appreciate and handle negative emotions, the more we can experience and enjoy positive ones. We experience love in direct proportion to the love that we give away.

Use emotions as springboards for accomplishing your life plan. What do you get excited about?

Emotions are present when we experience God's grace in the midst of tragedy, enjoy laughter and children's delight, feel the excitement of anticipation, suffer for doing right, hurt with a friend over a broken relationship, and rejoice in answered prayer.

We need balance to keep our strengths from becoming weaknesses: complacency may replace stability; dominance may replace generosity; distrust may replace discernment; and compulsion may replace responsiveness.

Invest your emotional energy wisely. As in anything else, our emotional energy is limited. Don't waste it on negative emotions, but rather, invest it where it will bring you the greatest return.

Chapter Challenge

Begin with the first challenge and work for thirty minutes. If you finish sooner, continue with the other challenges. Pick up the next day where you left off and spend thirty minutes proceeding through the list until each item has been completed.

1. Choose an area of your life where you lack the most emotional control.
2. Think through the consequences of not gaining control.
3. Go through the steps to gaining emotional control, specifically relating them to the area you have selected.
4. One month from now, evaluate yourself and determine if you have made any significant changes as a result of following the steps to emotional control. (I would love to hear of your progress!)

DEVELOPING SOCIAL SELF-DISCIPLINE

Jeff, a relatively new Christian, had a deep desire to share his new-found faith with others. But he kept getting signals that he was offending others, and he wasn't sure why. So he just chalked it up to resistance to the gospel. Jeff didn't realize that people were offended, not by his message, but by his presentation, his manners, and his inappropriateness in social situations.

For instance, Jeff was the one person people hoped would sit at another table at community socials. He had the disgusting habit of talking with a mouth full of food. And he always seemed to be talking! Too, he could be counted on to be the loudest and most boisterous person in attendance — and the things he said were often hurtful barbs disguised as humor. Yes, it was a sad day if Jeff chose your table! Maybe he did have some important things to say, but no one could get past his unappealing social flaws.

Why Is Social Self-Discipline Important?

All that we say and do as Christians reflects on the image of Jesus Christ that we give to the world. Just as a salesman represents his parent company, so do we represent the One who sends us. Think for a moment of the impression you receive from a company through the people that work there. Are they friendly and caring or abrasive and indifferent? Helpful and truthful or antagonistic and deceptive? Which kind of workers draw you toward the company? Which ones repel you?

As God's representatives to a dying and troubled world, we need to live in such a way that people will see that Jesus Christ can save and that He has come to give us life. The attractiveness of Jesus Christ needs to shine in every area of our lives.

Our social input often determines the depth of future friendships and relationships. Shallow, unattractive input weakens our future impact and in some cases nullifies it altogether. However, if we have become a pleasant aroma—the fragrance of life (2 Corinthians 2:15) to our sphere of influence—then God can more effectively use us in furthering His kingdom. And He often opens the door of our witness through social relationships that become meaningful friendships.

Compare two couples, Scott and Brenda and Eric and Marilyn. Both couples were committed Christians, both lived in the same neighborhood, and both were active in their community.

But there the similarities ended. Scott and Brenda were like a fine prism reflecting rays of light and beauty to others. They were gracious in social settings, thoughtful of others, and always seemed to know just what to say. People were attracted to them and wanted to get to know them better. They never lacked for friends. Through the friendships they nurtured, Scott and Brenda were able to point others to Jesus Christ as the answer to life's problems.

On the other hand, Eric and Marilyn seemed to repel people without even trying. They were brash, often cutting each other down in public. They were generally inconsiderate of people and were downright mean to some in particular. They turned people off by their lack of social graces, always seeming to blunder in their manners or conduct.

As a result, almost everyone shied away from them and they had few close friends, hence few opportunities to share their purpose for living on a deeper level. Even if they had had the opportunities, no one would have wanted to listen for fear their social awkwardness and ineptness would be catching. With self-control and social instruction, Eric and Marilyn could have changed the impact their lives were having on those around them.

Social self-discipline is also important because of the personal satisfaction we receive knowing we are equipped as fit representatives before the world. We acquire a boldness and confidence to move forward with the plans God has for our lives. Likewise, we do not have to be handicapped by indecision over simple formalities nor encumbered with a *faux pas* that could easily have been prevented.

Megan signed up for an etiquette course to polish and perfect skills she had learned as a little girl. She learned correct conduct, proper protocol, and social sensitivity. As a result, Megan took on a new appreciation of herself and exhibited grace and charm — qualities she had always admired in others.

Being disciplined in the social arena may also prevent bigger trouble in other areas — especially in the moral realm. James grew up in a very affectionate family, and he carried his affectionate ways into adulthood. After he married, James, unaware that his actions might be misconstrued, continued to touch whoever he was talking to. He had a magnetism that attracted others to him, especially women. In our society where people distance themselves from each other, James was meeting needs he didn't even realize were there. Some women's needs were so deep-rooted that his touch stirred up conflicting emotions in them. These led to an inordinate fixation on James, which led to marital discord for the women, who finally would pursue ungodly unions of which James was totally ignorant. That is, until one day one of the women showed up on his doorstep!

Social Etiquette

If you are lacking social graces, what can you practically do to improve in that area? First of all, your community may offer etiquette courses. The advantages of taking such courses are three-fold.

You learn by doing. Our daughter, Dione, took a one-evening course in an exclusive restaurant when she was nine years old. There was only one boy — and about ten girls — present. They learned what silver-

ware to use for each course, what to do with the napkin, how to ar-
range the silverware when you are finished eating, and proper manners. Their text was a five-course meal. (Dione even came home
and taught us some things!)

The young man was kept busy that night. Whenever one of the
young ladies needed to excuse herself to use the restroom, he was
taught to pull her chair out, remain standing until she returned,
and then seat her properly. The girls all wanted to have a turn being
treated in such a manner, so the young man was barely able to eat
his dinner. It was a learning experience that has left a favorable impression on Dione.

You will benefit from knowledge that took others years to learn and perfect.
Even if you don't absorb all the information, you will still be more
aware and knowledgeable than before. If the course lasts several
weeks, you will be able to chart your progress as well as make
friends with the other participants.

When I was a teenager, I attended a charm course with my sister.
We learned how to sit and walk properly, basic makeup techniques,
and hints on how to dress modestly with good taste. I didn't come
out transformed, but the professional manner in which the course
was presented impressed upon me the importance of social propriety.

*You may find your social fears abating as you gain confidence in knowing how
to conduct yourself in various situations.* Why turn down social invitations for fear of making a fool of yourself when you can take a
course to learn social skills or check out some library books on manners and social graces? Often the "want to" is there, but we just
don't know how to proceed. Books provide a wealth of information
that will enable us to learn the skills we lack. Then it's up to us to
put those skills into practice until they feel natural. And that takes
self-discipline.

It's a lot easier to do what comes naturally. But all of us can rise
above the status quo if we put forth the effort, and sometimes it doesn't
even require a lot of effort. The hardest part is taking that first step.

Another possible route for developing social skills is to ask for
feedback from someone whose social abilities you admire. Ellen

mustered the courage to ask for input from a woman who she respected in the church. It was the beginning of a long and valuable friendship. Not only did the woman help Ellen with her social skills, but she helped her with several other areas of her life as well. Ellen's first step in making some life changes came through asking for help in improving her social skills.

Social Essence

Social essence deals with the inner person, whereas social etiquette focuses on the outward. Anne was a very refined woman, successful in her field and highly respected for her accomplishments. Some had called her elegant and charming. She commanded attention wherever she went. By all outward appearances, Anne exhibited flawless social graces.

But those who knew her well had to admit that it was all for show. After a speaking engagement where she perfumed her speech with flattery and concern, Anne would turn around and criticize that same audience to her friends. She was caustic and self-righteous as she verbally shredded people to pieces. She complained about the measly fee they paid her. They should know better than to pay someone as well-known as herself such pittance. She would never accept an engagement with *that* group — even if they were national. They had better write her up in this month's magazine with a full-page color photograph, or she would broadcast to the world what an amateur organization they really were!

Anne's social essence did not measure up to her social etiquette. In fact, it totally negated her message and instead conjured up thoughts of disgust whenever her name was mentioned.

A person with a pleasing social essence will be thoughtful and kind — and not just for show. It will come from the heart. One's heart condition cannot remain hidden for long; sooner or later nuances will betray even the strongest effort to cover up the ugliness of his heart. Genuineness and humility characterize people whose concern extends beyond themselves. They exhibit courtesy and respect, and servanthood is their way of life.

What does your social essence say about your heart? Maybe you need to allow the Spirit of God to root out the ugliness and replace it with the love and beauty of Jesus Christ. Ask the Lord to show you one characteristic in this area that is not pleasing to Him, and then begin to work on it. You will first need to single out and become aware of instances where you practice this less-than-desirable trait. Then, with God's help, make an effort to change your habits and your heart.

Social Elocution

Our speech reflects our heart condition. "How can you who are evil say anything good? For out of the overflow of the heart the mouth speaks" (Matthew 12:34). With our tongues we can shred the insecure and slander the innocent.

Small high schools are breeding grounds for gossip. Because the student population is smaller, each one's life becomes open territory for the destructiveness wrought by the tongue. Ashley's family had just moved to town. She was an honor student, pretty, and a promising athlete. Needless to say, she caused a stir in the stomping grounds of the established popular crowd. Those with the most to lose took drastic action to protect their territory. Why, it was easy. All they had to do was slip in a tiny untruth here and there, ask an insinuating question, or threaten peer extinction if the other girls befriended Ashley.

Their tactics almost pushed Ashley to the brink of despair through anger and frustration at the helplessness of her situation. Fortunately, her parents saw what was happening and intervened, transferring her to a larger school.

Carl, insecure in who he was as a person, was devious nonetheless. Carl clutched at anything that masqueraded as a boost to his self-esteem. He tried them all—from belittling others to make himself look good to flattering those with social prestige to spreading juicy tidbits about those who threatened to command the spotlight. His tongue caused many heartaches.

James urges us to control our tongue (James 1:26), and Proverbs exhorts us to guard our tongues and therefore keep ourselves from calamity (Proverbs 21:23).

To improve social elocution, focus on being kind in your speech and sensitive to the feelings of others. Avoid sarcasm, eliminate gossip, and limit criticism. Concentrate instead on giving acceptance, affirmation, and appreciation.

Mary Jane is gracious in every way. An attractive woman in her thirties, Mary Jane has learned through the years the destructiveness of the uncontrolled tongue. Daily she listens to women whose lives have been ravaged by the insensitivity of another, reads about deep-seated hurts born out of thoughtlessness, and witnesses the struggles of adults still trying to cope with a parent's poisonous tongue.

By spreading encouragement and reaching out to others in their hurt, Mary Jane has experienced the powerful benefits of taming the tongue. She is blessed, her friends are inspired, and even mere acquaintances know that Mary Jane is a rare jewel.

Social Enrichment

Our social enrichment comes through our friendships and relationships with others. Without such interaction, our lives become shallow and self-centered. We can cultivate interpersonal relationships so that they bring joy and gladness to our lives, or we can trample them and sow tears and heartache.

Compare Dennis and Coleen, two professionals who work extensively with people. Dennis, a radio announcer, deals with the public on a daily basis. But people irritate him. He tries to keep his irritation from showing, but snide remarks escape from time to time. He is quick to judge and criticize his co-workers. He has an underlying need to be the best at everything, and he verbally abuses those who stand in his way.

His home life is no better. His family gets in his way, and he wishes he were single again. He blames people for making his life miserable, so he tries harder to isolate himself and begins to withdraw. But the more he withdraws, the more desolate his life becomes.

Coleen, a public relations specialist for a large firm, also comes in contact with many people each day. But Coleen thoroughly enjoys being with people, and it shows in both her public and private life. Those fortunate enough to be counted among her many friends feel specially chosen. And she doesn't make one friend feel more special than another—she has a way of making *all* her friends feel unique and wanted.

Coleen lives a rich and full life. Her friends are her dearest treasures, and she lets them know it often through her many deeds of kindness to them.

Friends are important. They help us determine who we are by giving us intentional, involuntary, and intimate feedback. This feedback helps us evaluate where we have been, where we are, and where we are headed. Likewise, when we give others feedback, we gain a measure of fulfillment not possible if we isolate ourselves. We are created for companionship, not for isolation. Classic Biblical examples of endearing friendships are: Ruth and Naomi (Ruth), David and Jonathan (1 Samuel), and Mary and Elizabeth (Luke 1).

A Few Words of Caution

Our appropriate or inappropriate social behavior will greatly influence how well accepted we are. If we ignore social taboos and protocol, we may find that others avoid us.

Katsie was out to grab all the limelight she could. At social gatherings she did away with propriety and snuggled up to the richest, most prominent people there. She made inappropriate remarks and refused to listen to the cautions of others.

Katsie barged ahead with her loud, attention-getting tactics, and on occasion acted shamefully. When people saw her coming, they quickly busied themselves or walked in the other direction. Katsie's brashness and insensitivity found her outside the very circles she so eagerly wanted to enter.

Although we need to develop satisfying friendships, we need to choose our friends carefully (Proverbs 13:20). Since it is impossible to be close friends with everyone you meet, choose friends that will encourage and motivate you to become the kind of person who pleases God.

Serve your friends, don't manipulate them. Use self-control in not smothering them or making them your clones. Friendships involve risk; betrayal among friends is not unknown. If a friend betrays you, cover their offenses with love. In love, also confront them about their behavior. There is risk, too, in being stretched beyond our comfort zone — but then, isn't most growth outside our comfort zone?

Summary

Social self-discipline may seem more trouble than it's worth. But you will be amazed at the difference it will make in your life. You will like yourself more, others will enjoy your company more, and you will not bring shame to the name of God.

Social etiquette focuses on manners and outward appearances. Anyone, regardless of background, can learn social graces. Enlist the help of a close friend or relative. Even small changes produce pleasing benefits.

Social essence involves inward character that one way or another will affect our acceptance, personal dignity, and our testimony to Christ's work on our lives.

Social elocution involves our speech — our choice of words and intensity of voice. It has been said that the serpent has the fastest moving tongue of any animal. Guard your tongue against evil.

Social enrichment results directly from the depth of our relationships. We were not created to exist in isolation. Many of our social habits have been learned; therefore, we can unlearn negative ones and build on positive ones. In allowing God to change us, we are often surprised at the intensity of enjoyment social relationships can bring.

Chapter Challenge

Begin with the first challenge and work for thirty minutes. If you finish sooner, continue with the other challenges. Pick up the next day where you left off and spend thirty minutes proceeding through the list until each item has been completed.

1. Ask God to point out a social area He would want you to improve.
2. Develop a personal plan to make those improvements.
   a. Take an etiquette course.
   b. Read a book pertaining to the area you are working on.
   c. Get information and feedback from a person you admire.
3. Ask God to give you opportunities for growth in that area, and practice what you have learned.

4. List five qualities you like in a friend. Work on these same qualities in your own life by choosing a concrete task each day to exhibit one of the qualities.

5. Work on deepening a friendship by accepting, affirming, and appreciating your friend. Be creative!

6. In two months evaluate yourself. Are you more fulfilled in your friendships and relationships?

EIGHT

DEVELOPING MORAL SELF-DISCIPLINE

Many readers will probably turn to this chapter first after scanning the table of contents. I have tried to point out in some of the preceding examples that even committed Christians can struggle with morality if they do not stay on guard. Morality extends into many aspects of our lives. In this chapter we will ask what moral discipline involves and look at some ways to develop it as part of our lives.

Moral discipline involves behaving according to a set standard that God has already given us through His Word. This fact in itself frees us from mind-boggling indecision and tempestuous wrestling with uncertainty. There are absolutes in Scripture that admonish us not to steal, lie, or commit adultery. Our problems begin when we try to rationalize our desires and resulting behaviors that run counter to the absolute. We slide into gray areas, sneak a little toe over the line, and convince ourselves we are not really going against the absolute in its strictest sense.

Each of us has the capacity to be morally corrupt; to be dishonest, sexually impure, or to harbor resentment and anger in our hearts. Lest we think that we are above being morally corrupt in a certain area, Scriptures warns us, "So, if you think you are standing firm, be careful that you don't fall" (1 Corinthians 10:12). And "If we claim to be without sin, we deceive ourselves and the truth is not in us" (1 John 1:8).

You may need to come down a notch or two and admit your pride over having not fallen. Realize that given the same background, circumstances, needs, and pressures of another, you too might have fallen. It is far better to face our inherent limitations and accept God's grace than to have to be shown how totally incapable we are of living a flawless life. Sure, we can contain our weaknesses for awhile (at least outwardly), but one day they may overwhelm us in ways we never thought possible — and in the areas where we thought we had the most control!

We are so quick to condemn others — and just as quick to justify ourselves. Why, our situation is unique! Suddenly, the moral codes by which we judge others do not apply to us.

Why Strive for Moral Control?

We need to go back to the foundation of our lives and determine why we want to be moral in the first place. Our ultimate motivation should be love for God and a desire to be more like Jesus Christ, not fear of retribution if we do not obey (though in the beginning we may often grit our teeth, since our desires consistently war with God's best for us).

Think for a moment. What has held you back from pursuing your own evil desires? Are you afraid of the consequences, concerned about your reputation? Or maybe you haven't come across just the right opportunity. Whatever the case, when we do encounter situations where our evil desires overwhelm us, it will take more than what has previously held us back if we are to win complete victory. God's power is available for us to overcome the enemy (1 Corinthians 15:57). But we have to *want* God to have the victory, and then we must cooperate with Him, even when it is the most difficult thing we have ever had to do.

Since God's Word assures us that He loves us (John 15:9), we know that His plan for us is ultimately better than anything we could possibly imagine. How often we are ready to throw away God's best in exchange for a lesser, temporary satisfaction! We believe that God could use a little help meeting our needs, so we jump at the first opportunity that looks inviting. But our hearts are desperately wicked and they deceive us. We convince ourselves of the rightness of a situation, only to find out later that it has destroyed us (Jeremiah 17:9; Proverbs 14:12).

Does fear or perhaps pride keep you clinging tightly to carnality? Do you fear you will be unable to do or give up what God requires of you? Then meditate on Philippians 4:13: "I can do everything through him [Christ] who gives me strength." Only as we allow God to control our moral selves will we experience the richness of His blessings in these areas of moral self-discipline. If we truly love God and desire to please Him, He will give us the grace and strength to overcome our sinful habits. And in the end, we will come to know Him more fully and will reflect more brightly the likeness of His beloved Son, Jesus Christ.

Identify Your Weaknesses

In order to combat moral weaknesses, we must single them out, name them, and admit that they are sin. Brushing away all the rationalizations, clearing away the convenient smoke screens that hide the truth, and taking an honest look at our motives may reveal some areas that have hindered us from living abundant Christian lives.

Now, at this point only the courageous will stay with me. Some may decide that the rationalizations and smoke screens provide too much security to let them go. But for those who honestly want to throw off the hindrances and disentangle themselves from the cobwebs of sin (Hebrews 12:1), the rest of this chapter is for you. May God bless you and assure you of His love as you embark on the following steps.

Getting Started

To get started, consider the following questions:

- Does anything in your life make you feel uneasy when you contemplate kneeling before the Lord and asking Him to bless your life?

- Is there a nagging thought or situation that isn't quite right but you don't know what to do about it so you do nothing?
- Is there a habit or practice your mind turns to in its free moments? What do you think about as you fall off to sleep?
- Could you meet anyone on earth face-to-face and know that everything is right between you?
- What has a hold on you—even a tiny one?
- Is there anything that takes the place of Jesus Christ in your life at any moment?
- What sins can you not tolerate in others?

Take a piece of paper and go over the questions once more, this time jotting down anything that comes to mind, even if it seems unrelated. Now go over the questions again, recording any thoughts that may have eluded you before.

Study your paper. Is a pattern developing? Organize each item you listed by category. For example, let's say your list looked like this:

What do I feel uneasy about?

—anger toward Jim
—relationship with daughter
—last credit card purchase
—the little lie I told yesterday

What situation isn't quite right, but I'm not sure what to do?

—situation with elderly mother
—resentment toward co-worker
—that person who is attracted to me

What do I think about when my mind is free?

—my boss
—how I can get more money in ways that no one will ever find out about
—how gracious the Lord is
—how I wish I had never done a certain thing
—what I want to accomplish
—how much someone has hurt me
—what heaven will be like
—not becoming like my mother or father

Is there any relationship that has not been made right?

—relationship with parents over unresolved conflict
—intimacy with a friend of my husband's
—the executive I get irritated with and treat unkindly
—a former teacher I never forgave for humiliating me

What has a hold on me?

—cigarettes, alcohol, drugs, or food
—a man or a woman
—money
—power
—hate
—sports

What takes the place of Jesus Christ in my life?

—television
—pornography
—a relationship
—money
—projects
—children

What sin can I not tolerate in others?

—flirting with opposite sex
—flaunting wealth
—irritability
—excessive control
—lying

Now on a separate sheet of paper list any of the above choices that have to do with money in one column. List other categories in successive columns—sex, anger, dishonesty, and so on.

After you categorize your own answers, you might find one column that is much longer than the others. This may be the area you need to start working on. (You should have identified a problem area if you were honest in answering the questions.)

Maybe all this is elementary to you. You already *know* your battlefield. You've been struggling with the same flaw for years. Whatever your situation, I assume that you have now isolated your weakness and sincerely desire to reverse the downward spiral.

Steps to Moral Decline

"I can never understand how people tell you things they have never told anyone after knowing you for only two minutes," my husband once told me. Speaking and living in various states has offered many opportunities to listen to the struggles of others. Over the years I have begun to see a specific pattern in the stages of moral decline.

First of all, there is a perceived need or desire. A deep longing, conscious or unconscious, exists within that often stems from a lack of a personal relationship with Jesus Christ. But becoming a Christian doesn't negate our other God-given longings. The problems arise when we try to meet those God-given needs and desires in our own ungodly ways. We are often driven by the needs we are trying to fulfill, but our relationship with Christ should affect how we choose to quench or fill those perceived needs. (Remember, sometimes our perceived needs are distorted.)

Denise grew up in a home where love was rarely expressed and where affection was almost non-existent. She could not admit it to herself, even after she was married, but she longed for affection even beyond what her husband was able to give. Denise had an underlying need to confirm her worth through the outward display of affection. As a result, when an understanding co-worker gave her frequent affirmations while putting his hand on her arm or giving her a pat on the back, she sought out ways for him to repeat and increase his affirmations. As is often the case, Denise began to be swept away by the current of an affair.

Secondly, after the longing tugs on our insides, we determine, whether consciously or subconsciously, to find our own way, instead of God's way, to meet that need or fill that desire. Ted had always desired to be rich. When he realized that his career was moving too slowly for him to attain that goal, he decided to figure out a way to speed things up. As an accountant for a large firm, he had access to company funds. Through cleverly rearranging figures, entries, and debits, he successfully increased his own bank account — that is, until one day he was discovered. Ted's desire to be rich clouded his perception, and his actions changed the course of his life. Had Ted thought through *why* he wanted to be rich, he would have discovered his weakness.

Ted was a very shy child who experienced frequent rejection. Somewhere along the way, he had acquainted acceptance and control of people with money. Even now, he was trying to get rich to impress a girl who didn't love him the way he loved her. He thought if he could only put aside enough money, he could win her favor. However, Ted's *real* need was self-acceptance, and he was trying to fill it by winning a girl's love, becoming rich to win that love, and then stealing in order to become rich.

Third, we start to make allowances for our behavior in order to justify ourselves to ourselves. Bess has struggled to keep balance and proper perspective in her career as a graphic artist. Having won numerous awards over the years, she has reason to boast. Part of her business necessitates self-promotion to convince her clients that she is capable of handling their accounts.

On the other hand, she is completely aware that her gifts and abilities come from the Lord, and she loves to boast about what the Lord has done in her professional life. In fact, she is sometimes awed by what He has done.

Over the years Bess would justify the boasting by telling herself that it was easier to explain to someone the nature of her business by showing them her portfolio (where her awards are displayed along with the samples of work). Bess needed to come to terms with the sin of pride, which is not the same as a healthy pride in one's work.

And she needed to ask herself if boasting in what the Lord had done was not a way of puffing herself up by insinuating that the Lord had been better to her than He was to someone else. (The first she was guilty of; the second she didn't think so, because she has dedicated her life to helping others find God's best for them.)

At what point did it become sin for Bess to discuss her accomplishments? For her, uneasiness after talking about her accomplishments usually indicated that she had overstepped the line. Now, for the most part Bess keeps her portfolio in the closet. She hands her clients a condensed bio and tells briefly, rather than shows, what her business entails, and then, only when asked. What perceived need do you think Bess was trying to fill?

The fourth step is a subtle flirting with sin. When those opportunities come (and they *will* come) to act on what we have already determined in our heart that we want, we begin by just dabbling. We think, *After all, there is nothing wrong with what I am doing. It is not a sin to just look (or hug or avoid telling the whole truth or take advantage of a certain loophole). Besides, there are people out there who are doing a lot worse than this! Hey, down deep I'm a pretty good guy, I just have normal drives like everyone else.*

We even argue with the Lord. "If You don't want this thing in my life, then take away the desire. Besides, I know You are bigger than any temptation that will face me even if I do get in over my head once in awhile."

We think we can handle a little temptation, convincing ourselves that we have a long way to go to actually sin. We allow a small compromise, rationalize our behavior, conceive of ways to increase similar opportunities, and deceive ourselves all the while.

Fifth, we ignore the conviction of the Holy Spirit. When we finally hear the Holy Spirit's warnings, it's usually after we have made more concessions than we had intended to make. At this point, we can continue to ignore the conviction or act on it. If we ignore God's voice, then the slide toward moral destruction accelerates unabated.

Steps to Moral Discipline

If you are currently in a situation that is not pleasing to the Lord, you need to take several specific steps.

First, confess your sin. Turn from your sin, and ask God to forgive you. He promises us in 1 John 1:9 that He will do just that. As far as God is concerned we are free to begin again.

Second, ask forgiveness. If you have wronged someone, you will need to ask their forgiveness and in some cases you will need to make restitution as well. Ask God for the opportunity, wisdom, and courage to proceed with this step.

Third, forgive yourself. Admit your feelings, your weaknesses, your frustrations, and your limitations with the situation. When we deny a problem exists, our eyes become blinded and we are unable to perceive reality. Acknowledge that you do indeed have a problem in your life to be reckoned with. Admitting our feelings to ourselves lessens their control over us. But we must then subdue any sinful feelings lest we unwittingly continue to nurture them and feed their fire in us.

Fourth, develop a mindset of being moral at all costs. Determine in your heart that you will not sin against God. Godliness is a choice of our will. Choose godliness. One pastor said that the garbage-in/garbage-out concept is understated. The garbage-in gets multiplied internally. An ounce of leavening (in Scripture leaven often symbolizes sin) produces one hundred pounds of fat dough. The mind translates garbage-in into one hundred different scenarios. There is a direct correlation between mental replay and moral failure.

We need to replace our thought patterns with God's thoughts, keeping our minds on things above (Colossians 3:2), taking every thought captive to make it obedient to Christ (2 Corinthians 10:5). Focus on the Lord, saturate your mind with Scripture, and do not allow fantasy to interfere with or replace reality.

Fifth, avoid presuming upon God's grace. One way Satan tempted Jesus in the wilderness was in this area. Jesus' response can be our response, too: "Do not put the Lord your God to the test" (Matthew 4:7). In other words, don't place yourself in a position where you have to depend on God's grace to get you out. Be cautious of potentially explosive situations. Run, flee, vamoose at the first hint of temptation. Don't entertain for one minute the thought that you can handle it this time.

But what happens if you can't flee? Joyce was in a position where it was almost impossible for her to flee. During those heart-wrenching months of increased sexual and emotional temptation, it seemed she spent more time on her knees than on her feet. Not only did she cry out for God's help, but she wisely implemented limits.

She tried to stay away from intimate conversations and refrain from sharing feelings or asking leading questions of a certain co-

worker. She avoided prolonged stares, any touching, or giving affirmations. Joyce also studied the signals she was sending and was
careful not to dress or act inappropriately. She used discretion, limited her time and contact with this particular man, and guarded
against the temptation to manipulate circumstances to be around
him. When she thought she couldn't hold out any longer and was
about to let down her defenses, God provided a way out. Her co-
worker was transferred to another city.

For some the way out may be moving, a loss of passion, an illness,
a change of job, or the grace to meet the challenge day after day. God
has promised us in 1 Corinthians 10:13 that He will not allow us to
be tempted beyond what we can bear. But we are still responsible
for obeying the Holy Spirit's warnings, setting up our defenses and
strategy for attack, operating within pre-determined boundaries
and limits, avoiding anything with immoral overtones, and being
careful not to cross over the line of acceptability in God's eyes.

*Sixth, ask God to show you what underlying, perhaps legitimate, need or needs
you are trying to meet by participating in or being tempted by the ungodly behavior.* One friend suggested that women need to be needed and
men need to conquer. Do you want for basics like food, work, or security? What about needs of beauty, companionship, love? Or perhaps your life lacks intimacy or purpose. Stop feeding the need
through ungodly means and allow Jesus Christ to meet your needs
in His time and in His way. Lean on Him for the strength to be
patient until He supplies. Don't allow yourself to be shortchanged
by accepting temporary satisfaction apart from God's best for you.

Seventh, practice accountability. One pastor told me that he thinks only
one out of about four hundred Christians practices the seventh
step, accountability. Christians tend to shun accountability. Why?
Perhaps they enjoy their sin and don't *want* to be held accountable.
Or, even if they would like a friend to see them through a difficult
situation, they don't like to unveil themselves and admit a character
flaw. Maybe they don't believe baring their souls to another brother
or sister in the Lord would make any difference anyway; it's a battle
they feel they have to fight alone.

Lloyd struggled with temptation in a certain area for months and was almost crushed by the weight of it all. Since he was in a Christian leadership position, he felt he could share his torment with no one. The warfare was so intense that he couldn't think straight. Finally, when he could stand it no longer, he confided in a fellow worker. The pent-up pressure came rolling off his back and with it a sense of relief he had not known during his long vigil with temptation.

Having unleashed the burden of his soul, Lloyd was able to back off from the situation, take a more realistic look, and think more clearly in order to develop an offensive strategy. The bond of friendship and fellowship deepened to fill some of the needs he was tempted to meet in ungodly ways. He felt someone understood him and loved him even with his human frailties. He had confidence that a brother would help fight the battle that almost made him go down for the third time. Lloyd was now answerable to someone in addition to the Lord. From now on, every action or thought would be weighed against the pain it might bring another brother who believed in him. The stakes were getting higher and, as a result, his motivation level for godliness also increased.

Eighth, set up a pattern of victory and chart your progress. The fallacy abounds today that we might as well give up trying after our first failure. The thinking goes something like this: *I already blew it, so why bother? Besides, that's just the way I am. I will never be able to change.* We get discouraged and go backward instead of forward.

One pastor friend said, "There is no escape for repetitive sin apart from repetitive confession. People think that since they already confessed the sin, and fell again, that they must not have been sincere. The enemy flogs them with their sin and makes them feel hypocritical. The antidote for sin is confession."

"We can't ever forget that God's grace is greater than sin. Although God's patience in time can wear thin, if our desire is to be holy, then in one sense God's patience is infinite."

Temptation will come even if your relationship in the Lord is healthy and growing. In fact, you can expect even more assaults if your life desire is to be holy. Satan will provide unlimited opportunities for you to fall with the underlying hope that you will disgrace the name of the Lord Jesus Christ.

We need to remember that being tempted is not a sin; sin results when we yield to the temptation.

For the longest time Angie berated herself for being attracted to a married man. She struggled in her heart and took it over and over again to the Lord. She had relied on the truths of Scripture and had victoriously avoided responding in a sinful way to temptation. But only when she saw that temptation in itself is not sin could she be free from the destructiveness of false guilt.

When we violate God's moral laws, we sin. Temptation appeals to our God-created needs and desires that are not evil in themselves but that scream to be met in ungodly ways. Only *yielding* to that temptation is sin, and yielding needs the consent of our will.

Recently our family and some friends celebrated our daughter's eighteenth birthday by tubing down a nearby river. In some places we could sit and relax and just flow with the current down river; however, in others we had to paddle with all our might to keep from being dashed against the rocks. Life is like that tubing experience. If we just allow the current to direct our course, we may float along smoothly for awhile. But in some situations we will be dashed against the rocks by giving in to temptation because we did not paddle against the current and move ourselves out of danger.

What are the dangerous currents in your life? Part of a good strategy for fighting temptation and developing moral self-discipline is determining what specific things you will do to combat your area of weakness. Make a list of everything that comes to mind that would help keep you from falling. For instance, someone who struggles with anxiety could avoid an overloaded schedule that creates pressure and strangles inner peace. A program of exercise also decreases tension and increases the body's ability to handle stress.

Perhaps some of you consistently give in to the temptation of placing money before all else in your life. The greed that ensnares you leaves you feeling wretched and unloved. But you can't seem to let go of your addictive quest for riches. You can start getting disentangled by making sure you give God a portion of all the money you acquire. Next, each month ask God to show you someone specific who needs financial help, and then ask Him for the willingness to share. It may be a widow fighting for survival for herself and three children. It may be the family hit by an unexpected illness. It may be the foreign student who will have to leave the country unless he can pay his tuition.

After writing down the things you can do to keep from being dashed against the rocks, make a chart listing each of the items. An example is given at the end of the chapter. Keep track of how often and in what capacity you make an effort to be godly in that area.

On another chart list all the ways you give in to your sinful habit. Then keep track of the days or hours in between each slip. We sometimes think that the battle is useless because we do not show perfection in overcoming it. But by charting your progress, you can see in black and white that you are becoming more Christlike in that area. Perhaps reward yourself in a predetermined way (not by allowing yourself to give in to the temptation you are battling, however) when you reach a certain goal. For example, if you war against losing your temper, your goal may be to go one day without acting out your anger in an inappropriate way. Upon your success you could treat yourself to a dinner out or purchase that new novel you have been wanting to read.

Ninth, live a life filled with praise and gratitude for what the Lord has done for you. As temptations come your way, praise God for them and allow the testing to become an opportunity to strengthen your faith and prove God's power sufficient. Praise Him for whatever comes to your mind throughout the day. Satan's arsenal is rendered less effective when we maintain a close walk with the Lord and accentuate it with praise.

Finally, help someone else who is wrestling with the same besetting sin that has caused you untold heartache. By virtue of your personal battle with the temptations in that area, you are in tune with the emotion, desperation, and even anguish of their struggle. You can show how Jesus Christ has helped you or is helping you to overcome and gain a measure of control in an area you previously felt was hopeless.

Life Is a Process

Prayer is fundamental to each of these steps. We cannot think for a moment that we will be victorious apart from God's power in us. Spending time on our knees bringing our lives, hearts, and minds into submission to the Lord Jesus Christ enables us to live in the power of His might. As we experience God working out His best in our lives, we will be encouraged to persevere, to have diligence in our journey to become what God would have us to be.

Jerry G. Dunn, a former alcoholic, outlines a cycle common to alcoholics in his book *God Is for the Alcoholic*. First of all, he becomes overwhelmed with the desire never to do it again. He's disgusted with himself and is sick and tired of failure.

Second, Dunn observed that after an alcoholic enjoyed the freedom of sobriety, he became proud and intolerant of other alcoholics. And third, just when he feels he has the problem under control, he succumbs to his buddies' urgings to take just one drink. From this point he can either go plunging into the depths of alcoholism or begin a slow decent to the same end. The cycle may take weeks, months, or years.

The cycle phenomenon may prove true for whatever moral battle you are fighting. Be warned. Moreover, I have noticed a different kind of cycle for vulnerability. Women especially seem greatly affected by cycles and tend to be more in control during certain weeks of the month. You may be more vulnerable at certain times of the year—tax season, holidays—or to certain stresses at the office. Perhaps even forbidden foods—chocolate, sugar, coffee—cause you to give up completely in other areas as well.

When two people who desire to be holy are fighting an immoral relationship, one is usually strong and can diffuse the danger of the moment. Another day, the other person may be the strong one.

Yet tragedy often strikes when one party gains a hard-won victory only to give it up willingly the next time rather than crush the other person by rejection, even if it is for their own good. How many men and women deny themselves freedom because they allow someone else to place them in bondage! Likewise, be careful that you do not enslave anyone in a similar way.

God uses moral struggles to develop maturity in our lives. We need to recognize our human liability and commit ourselves to continued learning and growing. Blessing will follow obedience. We must forget the past and reach for God's best. If we are to heal and begin again, we may need to rearrange our lives and accept the pain as the price of disobedience. And healing takes time. But remember also that our failures do not separate us from God's love (Romans 8:38).

Once we have been entrenched in a habit, it is far easier to do nothing than to alter our behavior. When you do decide to change, be prepared for spiritual warfare. Put on the whole armor of God (Ephesians 6:10–18). Memorize God's Word, concentrating on verses that speak to your needs.

Is it worth the effort? What good can come out of your struggle? Many can echo with me that you will come to know God in a deeper way, enjoying the richness of His fellowship with you. You will come to appreciate how God continuously meets your needs in His time and in His way. You will feel glad to be alive and to be a part of His kingdom. You will identify with the depths and heights of a fellow struggler. You will find discipline easier in other areas of your life. In fact, our sense of morality is foundational to our whole being. It involves our personal integrity, evidences our belief in the truths of Scripture, and shapes our future.

Life is a process. When does the final victory come and our struggle for moral purity end? Only when we see Him. Only then will we be truly like Him.

Barbara's Story

"I was raised in a home without affection and love, and I am still trying to make up for that lack. I never had a good relationship with my father. I missed all the emotional strokes a father can give: warmth, security, affection.

"A man at work who was almost twenty years older than me had just come through a divorce and would share his hurt with me. I am a caregiver personality and need to be needed, especially to help heal wounds. I looked for things in Ken that I missed from my own father. But somewhere along the way a new electricity changed the dynamics of our friendship.

"At first I thought I could maintain our friendship and control the other part of the relationship. But touching opened the next door — his hand on my shoulder, our closeness during a company meeting, even the brushing of his fingertips of my arm. Not big things. But they made me yearn for more. Females are tactile while men are visual. My mind exaggerated and replayed those brief encounters. I made excuses to be around him. I began to get bolder in my advances and acceptance of his advances. The pace and passion accelerated. It must have been pretty obvious to others in the office. But I was blinded by my own emotion and starvation for affection.

"At the same time, my own marriage began to deteriorate, and pressures from my job responsibilities increased. I felt smothered and wanted to escape. Eventually I did escape. . . .

"Although the affair was exciting, I paid my dues in untold emotional stress and heartache. I felt like a distortion in an otherwise normal world. I lost my self-respect and dignity. I was trapped in the ugliness of sin. I had disappointed the Lord, my husband, and myself. I felt sick.

"My momentary tryst didn't fit into my long-term goals and desires. When I saw the destruction I had allowed to come into my life, I decided to end the affair between Ken and me. I explained my decision to Ken and began to avoid him at work. It was hard to see the hurt in his eyes. I felt cruel and made concessions to try to ease his hurt. Then I realized what I was doing and knew that his hurt was a price I had to pay if I wanted to change.

"Every time I wanted to call I tried to postpone the urge. I told myself that tomorrow I would call. When tomorrow came, often the desire had passed. Time does a lot. If you take the boiling pot off the flame it has a chance to settle down for awhile and you are better able to control and evaluate what's happening.

"The frightening thing was that I found traits in Ken that I disliked in my husband. I sought out independence to find the ideal person. When you do that you are only fooling yourself. Your subconscious will find the same kind of person that you rejected.

"I had always needed an outward proof of my worth. That's what I was getting from the relationship with Ken. That first night after intimacy I woke up and for the first time in my life I felt like a woman. I felt pretty. Those things were important to me. I decided to work on those things to improve my self-image, thereby lessening Satan's hold on my life.

"I recognize that I will struggle with a seemingly bottomless pit that longs to be filled by other men's affection and affirmations. Now, I am almost cold in a friendship where I sense a potential danger. It's hard to maintain a distance for self-protection. A lot of fantastic men think I have no personality or excitement as a woman, and I know I am giving up some meaningful friendships. But, it's just like chocolate for some people—it's easier to have none than to have only a little and try to stop sensibly.

"I have also thought a lot about my relationship to Jesus Christ. There's no one in the world who has done as much for me as what Christ has done. I thought about the man Christ who died for me. That's significant. I don't know how I could have hurt Him. But, I did. And now, with His help I am beginning to put the pieces of my life back together again. It's hard, but I am finding happiness in the process."

Summary

Moral struggles transcend generations. We all have a bent toward particular weaknesses, whether jealousy, anxiety, sexual immorality, coldness and indifference, a complaining disposition, deceitfulness, pride, or greed. Satan has distorted legitimate, God-given needs to the point that we are mesmerized into meeting those needs in evil ways.

Our beliefs determine our thoughts, which contribute to our feelings, which often control our behavior. 1 Thessalonians 4:1-7 and 1 Peter 1:13-16 urge us to live a holy life; one sanctified (set apart) for the Lord.

We need to determine what is off limits for us. Hugging a friend in church may set off fireworks, both physically and emotionally. We may need to allow our mate to control the family budget because we can't be trusted with the checkbook. Or, we may need to avoid that relative who always gets us started drinking again.

Analyze your relationships and place yourself in a controlled environment. Sometimes we can wage war on our passions, be the victor, and then when we are not watching, fall harder than we ever thought possible.

It thrills me when I see righteousness and strength of character prevail. May the words of Titus 2:11–14 be ever true in your life!

> For the grace of God that brings salvation has appeared to all men. It teaches us to say "No" to ungodliness and worldly passions, and to live self-controlled, upright and godly lives in this present age, while we wait for the blessed hope — the glorious appearing of our great God and Savior, Jesus Christ, who gave himself for us to redeem us from all wickedness and to purify for himself a people that are his very own, eager to do what is good. Amen.

Steps to Moral Decline

- Perceived need or desire.
- Determination to meet need in our own way.
- Rationalizing our behavior.
- Flirting with sin.
- Ignoring conviction of Holy Spirit.

Steps to Moral Discipline

- Confess and turn from sin; ask God's forgiveness.
- Ask forgiveness of others if necessary; make restitution.
- Forgive self; admit problem; grieve loss.
- Develop mindset of being moral.
- Don't presume upon God's grace.
- Discover underlying need you are trying to fill.
- Make yourself accountable to someone.
- Chart your progress.
- Praise; give thanks.
- Help someone else who is struggling with the same weakness.

(Notice that there are twice as many steps to developing moral discipline as there are for slipping into moral decline.)

Sample — Chart A

Positive action steps to developing moral self-discipline in area of: **HONESTY**	Week #1	Week #2	Week #3	Week #4	Week #5	Week #6
Ask God, self and other person for forgiveness. Go back and tell the truth	*Tom at work* ✓ *neighbor* ✓ *mother on phone* ✓					
Accept consequence as part of learning process	*humiliation* ✓ *disappointment with self* ✓ *retribution* ✓					
Pinpoint areas of dishonesty	*lying* ✓ *deception* ✓ *exaggeration* ✓					
Determine what needs I am trying to fulfill	*self-worth* ✓					
Tell the whole truth — do not exaggerate	*told whole truth* ✓ *made eight sales* ✓					
Make myself accountable for improvement to a friend or mate	*talked to mate* ✓					
Dates I told the truth when before I would have lied or exaggerated	*7/16* ✓ *7/18* ✓ *7/20* ✓					
Praise God for progress, memorize Scripture on honesty, prayer for continued help	*7/16* ✓ *7/17* ✓ *7/18* ✓ *7/20* ✓ *Prov. 26:28* ✓ *7/17* ✓ *7/20* ✓ *7/21* ✓					
Rewards implemented when I reach my goal	*went to see a ball game* ✓					
TOTALS	**25**					

Sample — Chart B

Ways I give in to lack of discipline in area of: **HONESTY**	Week #1	Week #2	Week #3	Week #4	Week #5	Week #6
Rationalize to myself why something is not a lie	✔ ✔ ✔ ✔ ✔ ✔					
Don't tell the *whole* truth	at work ✔ ✔ ✔ at home ✔ ✔ ✔ ✔					
Deceive by insinuation	✔ ✔ ✔ ✔ ✔ ✔ ✔ ✔					
Steal items from office	staples ✔ ✔ paper ✔ pens ✔ ✔					
Be hypocritical: say one thing and do another	✔ ✔ ✔ ✔ ✔ ✔					
Wear a mask so others will think I have it all together	always! ✔ ✔ ✔ ✔ ✔ ✔ ✔ ✔					
Exaggerate	✔ ✔ ✔ ✔ ✔					
Outright lie to make myself look good or avoid unpleasant circumstances and consequences	✔ ✔ ✔ ✔					
Cheat on my income tax or expense reports	✔ ✔ ✔					
TOTALS	62					

Sample—Chart C

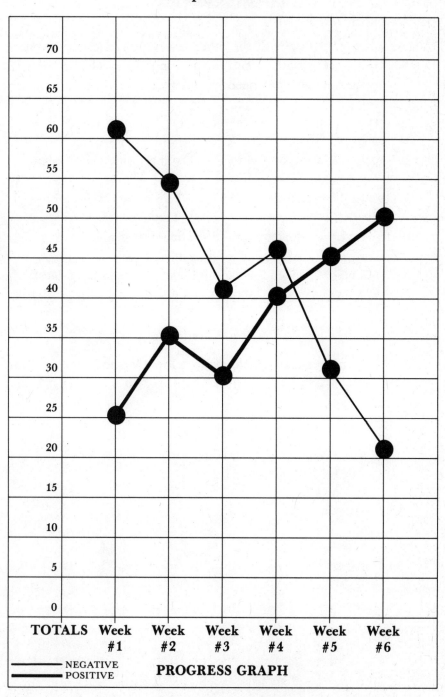

70

65

60

55

50

45

40

35

30

25

20

15

10

5

0

TOTALS   Week #1   Week #2   Week #3   Week #4   Week #5   Week #6

——— NEGATIVE
▬▬▬ POSITIVE   **PROGRESS GRAPH**

Chapter Challenge

Begin with the first challenge and work for thirty minutes. If you finish sooner, continue with the other challenges. Pick up the next day where you left off and spend thirty minutes proceeding through the list until each item has been completed.

1. Answer all of the questions under the section "Identify Your Weaknesses."
2. Choose one area you feel the Lord is impressing you to begin working on.
3. Go over the steps to moral decline. Where are you in that process for the weakness you will be working on?
4. Commit to developing moral discipline in that area.
5. Go over the ten steps to moral discipline. Start at number one. Continue on through the list until you know you have developed a measure of discipline in that area.

Advanced Challenge

Read one of the suggested books and allow God to use it in your life.

NINE

DEVELOPING FINANCIAL SELF-DISCIPLINE

No sooner had our crates arrived in Zaire than an African named Tatu was asking if he could buy our mini-bike when our three-year term was over. The mini-bike was barely visible among our other belongings in the four by four-foot plywood crate. Shocked at the request, Dave answered, "We'll see." Little did my husband realize the breadth of Tatu's appeal.

Some people think materialism is limited to the United States. But the longing for more indicates a heart condition inherent in fallen mankind. It transcends one's culture and economic strata. In this case, Tatu became first enthralled with the idea of possessing a mini-bike; then enraptured by the desire to have it; next, engulfed by the responsibility of owning it; and finally, enslaved to keeping it at all costs.

At the end of our term, Dave faced a difficult decision. Knowing how Tatu would have to sacrifice, not only to buy the mini-bike, but also to keep it operating, Dave hesitated to sell it to him at all. But because Tatu *did* ask him before anyone else, Dave felt obligated to honor the request.

A few years later we learned that the overwhelming desire to own the mini-bike had become Tatu's undoing. Not content with a bicycle that was within his means, Tatu brought disgrace to his family, lost his job and his home provided as part of his salary, and ended up losing the mini-bike after all.

Tatu had stolen money from his employer to pay for the mini-bike and gas. But as time passed, Tatu couldn't even use the mini-bike because parts weren't available. Tatu lost his dignity, respect from his family, and honor in the community — all for a thing. "Do not store up for yourselves treasures on earth, where moth and rust destroy, and where thieves break in and steal. But store up for yourselves treasures in heaven, where moth and rust do not destroy, and where thieves do not break in and steal. For where your treasure is, there your heart will be also" (Matthew 6:19–20).

Contentment

What about you? Are you content with your possessions? With your position in life? With your physical intricacies? All this time we have been talking about going beyond the status quo, bettering ourselves, and aspiring in our walk with the Lord. Why the contradiction in the financial area (at least it would seem so)? There is no contradiction when we understand the Biblical perspective on contentment. But we must first identify the underlying premise that we currently embrace to determine whether to pursue our direction or to change it.

If we espouse the world's basic premise, "Get all you can and keep all you get," then we would be hard-pressed to find contentment. But if we truly aspire to enhance our walk with the Lord, then we need to focus on what God says about contentment.

> But godliness with contentment is great gain. For we brought nothing into the world, and we can take nothing out of it. But if we have food and clothing, we will be content with that. People who want to get rich fall into temptation and a trap and into many foolish and harmful desires that plunge men into ruin and destruction. For the love of money is a root of all kinds of evil. Some people, eager for money, have wandered from the faith and pierced themselves with many griefs. (1 Timothy 6:6–10)

Keep your lives free from the love of money and be content with what you have, because God has said, "Never will I leave you; never will I forsake you." (Hebrews 13:5)

Therefore I tell you, do not worry about your life, what you will eat or drink; or about your body, what you will wear. Is not life more important than food, and the body more important than clothes? Look at the birds of the air; they do not sow or reap or store away in barns, and yet your heavenly Father feeds them. Are you not much more valuable than they? Who of you by worrying can add a single hour to his life?

And why do you worry about clothes? See how the lilies of the field grow. They do not labor or spin. Yet I tell you that not even Solomon in all his splendor was dressed like one of these. If that is how God clothes the grass of the field, which is here today and tomorrow is thrown into the fire, will he not much more clothe you, O you of little faith? So do not worry, saying, "What shall we eat?" or "What shall we drink?" or "What shall we wear?" For the pagans run after all these things, and your heavenly Father knows that you need them. But seek first his kingdom and his righteousness, and all these things will be given to you as well. (Matthew 6:25-33)

Examine Your Attitudes About Money

What do you really think about money? Are you afraid of it? Enamored by it? Frustrated by lack of it? Have you become its slave or have you become its master? Ours is a world where, even in remote civilizations, a system of value exchange is necessary; whether it be an exchange of dollars for dresses or monkey skins for machetes. Since it would be hard today to exist without such a system of exchange, we must cultivate the proper attitude toward it. Without the mindset of living by financial faith, we will soon find ourselves in financial bondage, whether we are enslaved to creditors or chained by our own passion to acquire more and more.

Kristin and Kirk were in financial bondage. Although they made good salaries in the early years of their marriage, they felt they deserved the best of everything, and they were determined to have it all now. It seemed very painless really — from squandering their wedding money to feeling important having three credit cards to the red carpet treatment of stores' in-house credit plans. Kristin and Kirk knew they could pay for everything later and enjoy it in the meantime.

But they weren't expecting the bundle of joy that left Kristin weak and unable to return to work. Now what were they to do? Kristin and Kirk began to fight more frequently. Now the things they had bought on credit created bitterness whenever they looked at them; that new dining room set, the big-screen television, the latest kitchen appliances. Kristin would give them all up to have peace and fun restored to their marriage. But the future looked grim.

Kristin and Kirk did finally become free from their financial entanglements, but only after cutting up the credit cards, implementing a plan to keep from going further into debt, and living for years without buying anything other than bare necessities.

Financial bondage causes disillusionment, bitterness, insecurity, anxiety, loss of sleep, envy, ungratefulness, enslavement, and fear. And it all begins with our attitude toward money. If financial bondage brings with it so many negatives, what is the underlying pull that would cause us to allow financial enslavement in our lives?

First of all, we need to look beneath the surface and ask ourselves, "What need are we trying to meet by overspending? Is it to support a sagging self-image? Pretend power and prestige? Dissolve depression and dissatisfaction? Pamper with pointless pomp? Or fascinate fake friends?"

When we have admitted that we are trying to meet our needs in ungodly ways, we then should commit to a life-change in our hearts and live by financial faith.

Make sure your heart is right with God in every *area of your life.* Cindy was a single mother with two young children. After paying for day care, she didn't even have enough money to cover her living expenses. She had thought about serving God in every area of her life. But for her it just wasn't practical. You see, there was a way Cindy figured she could make ends meet.

For one thing, she completely cut out giving to the church. And then there was her bread-making business. Oh, she knew she didn't have the proper health and business licenses, but after all, doesn't

God help those who help themselves? The only thing was, she had a sick feeling every time she sold a loaf of bread. And she lived in fear that one day she would be caught and fined.

Not only that, but Cindy had bouts of depression that incapacitated her for weeks. It was all she could do to survive. She wouldn't have had the energy to serve God even if she had wanted to.

What Cindy didn't realize was that God is very concerned about our needs and even knows them before we ask Him (Matthew 6:32). But God is also concerned about our lives honoring Him in every way. And that includes being honest and submitting to the laws our government has placed over us (Romans 13:1-7).

Honoring God in every area of our lives does not insure financial wealth and freedom from life's problems. What it does insure is a clear conscience, a clean heart, and a close relationship with the Lord.

Realize that all we have comes from God (John 1:3; Job 41:11). If we are convinced that everything we have belongs to God, then some things will be true about our attitude toward money:

- We will be generous with what God has entrusted to us.
- We will take steps to insure that we are using our resources as God directs.
- We will not be preoccupied with the acquisition, disbursement, or availability of those resources, but rather view them as a tool to accomplish God's plan for our lives.

After years of trying to make it to the top, Les had finally arrived. Sure, he lost his family and friends in the process, but now they would have to admit he was somebody great after all. And, you're right, he had been very selfish over the years. Okay, he even used less than honest tactics. But he had made it!

However, before Les had much of a chance to bask in his self-made victory, his world crashed around him. The stock market plummeted, and Les lost his fortune in the span of twelve hours. Never had he despaired as he did now. Gone! Everything he had worked for was gone! And he didn't even have the support of his family and friends to see him through this awful time.

It was then that Les came face to face with the fickleness of wealth. It could be here today and gone tomorrow. It was never really his after all. Les had given up the real for the superficial (Matthew 16:24–26).

Know you are in God's will and be faithful to it. Bruce's unhappiness at work grew until he felt he could stand it no longer. He had been hired as a charter pilot. Bruce loved to fly and he had been content and grateful for his job.

But the charter department did not bring in the needed revenues to justify keeping or expanding it. Now the sales department . . . well, it pulled its weight! So, in the end, the charters faded into oblivion and Bruce found himself behind a desk in sales. He was a valuable employee, so the company offered him this new position along with a substantial raise.

As the weeks grew into months, Bruce felt dissatisfaction and frustration mounting. He knew he was doing his best for this employer, but sales just weren't his bag. And he missed being in the cockpit. Maybe he should reconsider. Was this really where God wanted him right now?

A few weeks later another corporation offered Bruce a position as a pilot. The peace Bruce felt about accepting the offer reassured him that God was leading him to leave his current employer.

Whether it concerns owning a certain piece of property, working for a certain company, or participating in a certain activity, we need to concentrate on being in the will of God. If we purposefully disobey what we feel God would have us do, then we can't expect Him to bless in the financial areas of our lives.

Maybe we are convinced we are in the center of God's will working where we do. But we also need to be faithful in doing the best job we can for God's glory. Are we faithful in representing Jesus Christ in our appearance, attitudes, and actions?

Turn your finances over to God by an act of your will. Although Sheri and Doug were convinced they couldn't exist on Doug's salary alone, Sheri was just as convinced that she should stay at home with their three children. Even at the peak of their frustration Sheri and Doug felt their only alternative was to trust God totally for their financial dilemma. In addition to taking the other steps to living by financial faith, they jointly decided as an act of their will to allow God free reign in the area of finances and to be obedient to His leading.

Putting the children first, Sheri continued to stay home. Little by little Sheri and Doug made their way through the maze of financial uncertainty. God gave them peace that He would provide if they were faithful to His will for them. And He did provide in amazing ways. On paper they never seemed to have enough, but somehow they met their bills on time. Doug found odd jobs here and there, and Sheri took care of a neighbor's child a few days a week. And through it all, Doug and Sheri enjoyed a deeper and more satisfying relationship.

Tithe faithfully. Much has been written about the tithe. Whether you hold to a strict 10 percent or a larger or smaller portion, the important thing is that you honor God by the first fruits of your income (1 Corinthians 16:2). This kind of honoring begins in the heart. We can tithe 30 percent begrudgingly or 5 percent out of devotion and sacrifice. Which do you think is more pleasing to the Lord?

During one particular two-year period in our marriage, finances were even tighter than usual. Dave felt our first responsibility was to meet our monthly obligations rather than tithe regularly. He reasoned that not to meet them would be a poor reflection on Jesus Christ. So, over that two-year period we tithed sporadically and only after the bills were paid. And there never seemed to be enough to meet even our basic living expenses.

Then, Dave changed jobs and we moved to another state. We decided that we would tithe faithfully, even if it looked as if we wouldn't have enough to meet the bills. It's amazing what happened over the next year or so. Through unforeseeable (to us) events, Dave was unemployed for eleven out of fourteen months. During that time God faithfully and miraculously met *every* need we had. We were shocked one day to receive a one-thousand-dollar check in the mail from a longtime friend in Alaska who was himself unemployed at the time! What an awesome God we serve!

Praise God for the lean times as opportunities to build your trust in His character. During that fourteen months, we saw door after door close to potential employment. From time to time Dave found odd jobs to keep us going for awhile. But the critical value that experience had for us was this: we learned first-hand that our security rests not in a position, employer, or even the government, but in the Lord. We learned that no matter what our state of affairs, God is faithful.

This lesson removed the anxiety and fear that are so often present at the thought of losing a job. God brought us through, we grew closer as a family, and the children were able to see direct answers to prayer almost continually for that fourteen months.

Pray instead of connive or go into debt. Since God knows our needs before we ask, the greatest lesson we must learn is to wait patiently for Him to supply in His time. Perhaps your car won't run and you don't have the money to get it fixed. Instead of rushing out to the nearest car dealer, pray as a family for either the finances to fix it, an alternate means of transportation, or confirmation that He in fact wants you to purchase another vehicle. There are creative alternatives to our dilemmas. In this case, maybe you could take a bus to work and use your commute time more wisely than sitting in rush hour traffic. God may have wonderful things in store for you through the people you meet each day. Or perhaps you could carpool with several co-workers.

For a time, you may have to humble yourself and ask the assistance of your friends and neighbors. Americans have become so self-sufficient and private that we are closing out opportunities for growth and enrichment through the lives of others. We have some neighbors whom we have seen only a handful of times, and then only through the window. They have an electric garage door opener and rarely venture outside. We know they still live there because we see their car coming and going.

During the time that our vehicles were malfunctioning, we were forced to ask our neighbors for help. Doing so gave an opportunity to develop warm friendships. And we realized how special it is even to have one car. It was then we decided to try to change our lifestyle to accommodate only one car instead of two. For now it has worked very well. We combine trips, save on gas and insurance rates, and do more things together instead of going our separate ways in separate cars. We have seen God supply over and over when we have allowed Him the freedom to do so.

Lean on God's promises. In my business I have great freedom to set my fees. Since I have very little overhead working from my home, I don't have to charge as much as the industry rates. On the other hand, if I undercharge, it creates more difficulties for others in the same profession. Those are the facts. But the heart of the matter is that (for me) I am in business to represent Jesus Christ to only those with whom I come in contact. At the same time I take on only those projects that I feel God would have me do.

One day I decided that I would change my fee structure to reflect my purpose for being in business. After explaining that purpose to my clients, I shared with them the new fee structure. They were to pay me, after completion of the project, what they perceived my work was worth to them. I have found that most clients are very generous. And they feel good about paying me and showing their appreciation for the work I do for them.

I respect John MacArthur for his stance on receiving income from speaking engagements. His policy (according to one of his radio messages on finances) is not to charge a fee for speaking. If, however, the group chooses to give him something, he accepts it, thanking God for being the source of the gift.

God has promised to supply all of our needs (Philippians 4:19). It may not be through conventional means. Maybe a friend will give us *just* the item we need, or a door will open up in an unusual way.

I have a long-term back injury for which swimming has proved to be the most beneficial treatment. However, in the winter, I really hurt. So, one year I asked the Lord to provide a pool for winter use. Several doors opened which allowed me a complimentary membership to an exclusive health club with an indoor heated pool. (Of course the spa, sauna, and weight room weren't bad either!)

If we really believe that God will supply all of our needs, then our actions will attest to it in creative ways. And the world will take notice, bringing glory to our Father who is in Heaven.

Allow God to teach you spiritual lessons through correlations in finances. In my life there is a classic example of a lesson I have never forgotten which has become a foundational principle for me. We had been married about five years and had two small children. At the time Dave was in school taking an intensified aviation course. Our food budget was eighty dollars a month. Because we enjoyed entertaining and considered it to be a ministry, we had many families over each month. These were struggling students who most often had less income to live on than we did. So there was a two-fold purpose for having so many people for dinner.

One month I decided that I was going to try to stretch the grocery money a *lot* further and invite no one for dinner that month. After three weeks the money and the food ran out, and we ate oatmeal, without milk, for the last week. It was many years before I could enjoy oatmeal again!

How graphic of the Lord to show us that if we give with open hearts and hands, He will supply. But when we become self-centered and stingy, He withholds his blessing. This has proved true in our lives time and time again!

Maybe God is trying to get your attention through the lack or even abundance of money and material prosperity. Be alert to His call even in the seemingly insignificant circumstances.

Determine a budget and gain self-control over your spending. There are many helpful books on the market which deal with Christian finances, and I have listed several in the suggested reading. It all goes back to planning. A plan gives us a guide that helps chart our course. After making a budget, determining to stick to it is an act of the will. There will be unforeseen expenses, opportunities, and crises. Ideally, we should plan for these. However, if your life has been as unusual and varied as ours over the years, then you may find it next to impossible to plan adequately, and even more difficult to make finances stretch.

This brings us to an issue that most authors avoid. Everyone knows that budgets are supposed to work out practically on paper and intellectually. However, we have found another principle at work here. We have lived for many years depending on God to provide the job and to meet the needs that went beyond the salary. Most books insist on the necessity of saving a portion of your income each month. That's great, IF you can do it. So often we could barely pay our bills, let alone set aside something for savings. (And I'm talking a *no-frills* budget!)

If we had extra money, we would intend to put it in savings and sometimes it even got there. But, invariably, if we had an abundance, God would show us someone who needed it more *right then* than our savings did. No, we don't have much of a savings account, but we have been faithful and obedient with what God has given us. Each of you will have to determine in your own heart God's financial plan and priorities for your life. There have been times when we had unexpected needs for perhaps thousands of dollars. And God has been faithful *every time* in meeting those needs. What a testimony to our children of the practical faithfulness of the living God!

Another issue I would like to address deals with the wife's dilemma. God requires that the wife be ultimately submissive to her husband in financial matters (Ephesians 5:22). However, she may not always agree with his priorities for spending. But over the years God has blessed the willing relinquishing of my control to Dave. (And sometimes not so willing.) I would often see the wisdom of his decisions at a later date.

One particular instance took place when we were on deputation to present our work to churches before going overseas. We had visited one church where there was criticism about our taking three spatulas instead of one or two. (We were going to be in the jungle for three years and I used spatulas all the time. Should one break, melt, or get lost, I wouldn't be able to replace it.) This experience warned me about the seriousness of using deputation funds *very* wisely!

So, here is Dave wanting to spend hundreds of dollars on two mini-bikes to take overseas for our ground transportation. I thought *very* strongly to myself, "That is the stupidest waste of money! I can just imagine what people will think!" I had never been on a mini-bike and I certainly didn't see any use for it now. Since I had recently been learning more about the wife's submission to her husband, I decided not to say anything. But inside I was totally against buying the bikes.

Once in Africa, I saw the wisdom of Dave's decision. In fact, the mini-bikes were absolutely the best possession we took with us. They vied for practicality with my typewriter and sewing machine. I would gladly have left the spatulas and most of my clothes behind if I had had to choose between them and the bikes.

The girls were small enough to ride two with Dave and one with me. We took picnics to nearby villages, enjoyed Saturday afternoon jaunts in the jungle, and used the bikes for the many errands crossing from one side of our large station to the other. Dave and I would have a blast going on long rides in the rainy season. We would come back covered with mud from head to toe. The bikes wouldn't even be recognizable. We had the opportunity to see a large section of our corner of Zaire that we wouldn't have otherwise been able to see or experience.

In addition, the mini-bike was my ticket to freedom when the stress of the day would begin to overtake me. I would trek on down to the grass airstrip, making sure that no planes were expected, and ride the bike with the throttle wide open (all of thirty-five miles an hour). With the sun on my back and the wind in my face, worries would cascade off with ease, leaving me refreshed to finish the day. Yes, buying the mini-bikes was one of the smartest decisions Dave has ever made!

Financial Peace

Peace in financial matters sometimes comes only after obeying what we know God would have us do. One sensitive area for most couples deals with financial freedom to spend a small portion of a paycheck without having to answer to one's spouse. After twenty years of marriage, we finally have this one worked out.

I felt a need to have control over a part of the budget without having to give account. So, instead of just writing a check for groceries, I have a portion out of each paycheck. The further I make the grocery money go, the more I have to spend on gifts, a lunch out, or a new book. Ideally, Dave should have the same privilege. But with two kids in a Christian school and one in college, Dave has a hard time spending on anything beyond necessities, unless it is for someone else.

But, you know, even in the amount that is left from groceries, God still has a say. When I buy a gift for one of the girls or for someone else, or want to do something special with the money, I get advance clearance from the Lord. And the still small voice or uneasy conscience or heartfelt peace usually gives me a pretty good idea whether to go ahead with a purchase—large or small or even very small. Listening to God's voice within offers a freedom and a confidence that what I am doing is pleasing to Him.

At times I have chosen not to make a purchase because I didn't want to spend the money right then. Later, I would realize the foolishness of my decision because I would end up paying more for the same item or wouldn't be able to find another gift as fitting.

Building some financial freedom into the budget, even a few dollars a month, enables us to have some relief if money is scarce. Some of the best investments we will ever make are those small deeds of kindness we do for someone else—a card, a small gift, a lunch out. But we need freedom built into our lifestyles to do so, or we will feel guilty with every penny we spend.

Maybe what you have to share with someone would seem small in the world's eyes. But that is not important. You are sharing a part of yourself, and it will be meaningful to you and hopefully to the receiver. While we were on deputation, a church wanted us to post a list of the things we would need. On that list was a box of paper clips. Two elderly sisters had their heart in missions, but the only thing they could afford to give was the box of paper clips. I'll tell you, those paper clips meant a great deal to us!

In addition to being a blessing to others, giving enables us to hold our possessions and wealth loosely. We can learn as Paul, "I know what it is to be in need, and I know what it is to have plenty. I have learned the secret of being content in any and every situation, whether well fed or hungry, whether living in plenty or in want" (Philippians 4:12).

Sometimes we become so concerned with pinching our pennies that we do not allow God the freedom to dilate our dollars. I am reminded of the principle found in Leviticus 19:9–10: "When you reap the harvest of your land, do not reap to the very edges of your field or gather the gleanings of your harvest. Do not go over your vineyard a second time or pick up the grapes that have fallen. Leave them for the poor and the alien. I am the Lord your God." I remember the times (although short-lived) when I felt it was my Christian responsibility to pinch pennies until they almost bled to death. I didn't enjoy living that way, and it kept me from smelling the roses along the way.

When I came upon this example in the Old Testament, I likened my freedom in sharing to the gleanings of our harvest. We can become so preoccupied and obsessed with clipping coupons, calculating costs, and cutting corners, that we forget our purpose in wisely managing our resources: to be faithful in using what God has given us to work out His plan in our lives.

There is one caution I would give concerning money. Seen most often among missionaries and over-conscientious Christians, in our student days it was dubbed "poor-mouthing." This is the scenario whereby a person takes a great deal of pride in how little they spend for food, clothing, housing, or any other commodity. It gives way to boasting and usually only fools the person engaging in it. In our earlier years we were guilty, but we soon realized how awful it really sounded. How much better it is to praise God for His provisions than to focus on ourselves through boasting.

Several Scriptures bring us full-circle to our outlook on finances:

This is what the Lord says: "Let not the wise man boast of his wisdom, or the strong man of his strength or the rich man boast of his riches, but let him who boasts boast about this: that he understands and knows me, that I am the Lord, who exercises kindness, justice and righteousness on earth, for in this I delight," declares the Lord. (Jeremiah 9:23–24)

Then I realized that it is good and proper for a man to eat and drink, and to find satisfaction in his toilsome labor under the sun during the few days of life God has given him—for this is his lot.

Moreover, when God gives any man wealth and possessions, and enables him to enjoy them, to accept his lot and be happy in his work—this is a gift of God. He seldom reflects on the days of his life, because God keeps him occupied with gladness of heart. (Ecclesiastes 5:18–20)

Command those who are rich in this present world not to be arrogant nor to put their hope in wealth, which is so uncertain, but to put their hope in God, who richly provides us with everything for our enjoyment. Command them to do good, to be rich in good deeds, and to be generous and willing to share. In this way they will lay up treasure for themselves as a firm foundation for the coming age, so that they may take hold of the life that is truly life. (1 Timothy 6:17–19)

Summary

For many, financial self-discipline does not come easily. The trappings of a glittering, empty world often leave no resources for the things of the Lord. Others would love to give more to the Lord's work but are frustrated in even trying to make ends meet.

Whatever your situation, God has called us to have an attitude of contentment in our heart for what He has given and what He has withheld. Living a life of financial freedom involves living by financial faith.

How to Live by Financial Faith

- Make sure your heart is right with God in every area of your life.
- Realize that all we have comes from God.
- Know you are in God's will and be faithful to it.
- Turn your finances over to God by an act of your will.
- Tithe faithfully.
- Praise God for the lean times as opportunities to build your trust in His character.
- Pray instead of connive or go into debt.
- Lean on God's promise.

- Allow God to teach you spiritual lessons through correlations in finances.
- Determine a budget and gain self-control over your spending.

Chapter Challenge

Begin with the first challenge and work for thirty minutes. If you finish sooner, continue with the other challenges. Pick up the next day where you left off and spend thirty minutes proceeding through the list until each item has been completed.

1. Ask God to show you any wrong attitudes you have about money.
2. What emotional needs do you try to meet through money, either by spending or hoarding it?
3. Ask God to show you ways in which you lack control in your spending.
4. Set up a budget.
5. Make a personal commitment to live by financial faith.
6. Follow the steps to living by financial faith.
7. Simplify your life in some way.
8. Pray for resources and opportunities to give.

Advanced Challenge

Choose one of the books for suggested reading and read it, allowing God to use it in your life.

TEN

DEVELOPING SPIRITUAL SELF-DISCIPLINE

H ave you ever met people who glowed? Who seemed to be set apart from the masses of the world? Who could grace a crowd with their humility and at the same time possess a quiet strength rarely seen except among the great?

I have a friend who exhibits such characteristics. Lynne has a smile that draws you in its embrace, eyes that convey care and concern, and words that reassure and inspire. There is an essence about her that makes people marvel at her inner character. It has been said that if a person spends time with the Lord, they won't have to tell you, for it will show in their life. Lynne's life reflects Jesus Christ in that way.

Several years ago Lynne began to cultivate an intimate relationship with Christ. It was then that Lynne's outward life began to change. Her speech took on an angelic quality, her appearance acquired a new dignity, and her many deeds of kindness attested to her deepening love for people.

These changes were not something contrived, bought, or preplanned. They came gradually, some quicker than others. They came through the supernatural working of the Holy Spirit in

Lynne's life. Lynne's individuality was strengthened. Her unique-ness and fresh outlook on life caused others to examine their own lives.

The Importance of Spiritual Self-Discipline

Christ-like character and conduct will result as we make an effort to develop discipline in our spiritual lives. There will be an outward separation from the world. This is not an isolation whereby we close ourselves off from the needs of the world. Rather, it is a life-style that states, "This is a person with integrity, self-control, and compassion. His focus is not on himself and what he can acquire, but on helping others, fulfilling God's plan for his life, and being courageous in the face of difficult circumstances. His life shows that he lives by a different value system."

Conrad felt that his life was set apart for God's use. In keeping with this belief, Conrad took steps to alleviate certain encum-brances from his life, such as the unethical practices at work. He knew that by taking a stand he would risk not only his job but valu-able contacts in his field as well.

Conrad also thought his family should be more set apart in their home life. As a result, Conrad and his wife decided to sell their tele-vision set. They soon realized that removing the television from their home was one of the best decisions they had ever made for their family.

The kids began to read books and magazines that they had no time for before. They even developed an interest in news maga-zines and books far beyond the norm for their age. The family spent more time having fun together, whether it was for trips to the park or board games while eating popcorn in front of a fire. They even participated together in service projects for the homeless. Conrad and his wife also noticed that their relationship took on a more interesting and meaningful dimension.

As Conrad looked at other areas of his life, he made subsequent changes—from the way he spent his money to the way he invested his time to even the thoughts that occupied his mind. And he never felt more satisfied and fulfilled. God had given spiritual blessings in abundance. No, it was not always easy, but Conrad was convinced that for him it was the *only* way to live!

God requires that each of us be set apart for his glory. The cost may differ from one person to another, but the requirement is the same.

Even as I write this, our eighteen-year-old daughter is facing an ethical dilemma many miles away at college. Her boss has instructed her to lie outright. Jeannette has only been working there one week and really needs the money to finish paying for this semester's room and board. She has already determined not to lie — but lying is only one of the unethical practices going on around her.

How far apart should she set herself? Should she quit, not exposing herself to perhaps illegal situations? Should she take a stand and tell them that she doesn't condone what they are doing, and continue working there (provided she doesn't get fired first)? Or should she be more aggressive and perhaps have someone check into the areas where she knows there is wrongdoing?

Dave has handled the situation with wisdom. He has shared with her our opinions in the matter but urged her to go before the Lord and determine what is right for her. She will be responsible for her own decision. At any rate, we think that this will be a growing experience for her. Should she decide to quit (or be forced to), then she will need to trust the Lord, either for another job or else for school funds to be supplied by another means.

Another evidence of spiritual discipline is an inward transformation of character qualities. Where once there were bitterness and anger, peace and joy will reign. Where once there were greed and selfishness, generosity and love will prosper. Where once there were lust and addiction, self-control and freedom will have the victory.

These changes cannot take place without a personal relationship with Jesus Christ (see John 3:16) and a willingness to submit to the authority of His control in our lives.

> Therefore, I urge you, brothers, in view of God's mercy, to offer your bodies as living sacrifices, holy and pleasing to God — this is your spiritual act of worship. Do not conform any longer to the pattern of this world, but be transformed by the renewing of your mind. Then you will be able to test and approve what God's will is — his good, pleasing and perfect will. (Romans 12:1-2)

Spiritual Disciplines

Elsewhere we have discussed spiritual disciplines such as fasting, early rising, memorizing Scripture, and giving. Here we will focus on several others, although the list is not necessarily all-inclusive. This is not intended to be a theological discourse but rather an emphasis on basic disciplines necessary for spiritual health.

Self-discipline is not more important in one area than another, but I believe that by exhibiting spiritual self-discipline we gain strength and inner fortitude to meet the challenges in other areas of life.

The Word of God

Beginning with the Word of God, we focus our thoughts on Jesus Christ, who He is, and His desire to work in us. Through God's Word we learn of the precepts, will, and mind of God. We learn of our shortcomings and sins as well as our spiritual blessings in Christ Jesus. The Holy Spirit opens our understanding and increases our faith by hearing the Word of God (see Romans 10:17).

Although Greg was a sincere Christian, his life remained rather stagnant until he began to conscientiously read and study the Bible. As he gained an understanding of who God is and the kind of relationship that He wanted with Greg, Greg began to grow, and his outward actions became more Christlike.

The inner man evidenced a change as well. Greg displayed a humble spirit that accepted God's control over his life. Actually, there was freedom in relinquishing control. His heart was lighter and he no longer tried to carry the burdens that threatened to overwhelm him. In making decisions, Greg began to trust in God's wisdom rather than his own.

Daily Bible reading and study will intensify our spiritual growth (see 2 Timothy 3:14-17; 1 Peter 2:2); meditating on that Word will insure our personal success (see Psalm 1:2-3); and memorizing God's Word will inspire our personal purity (see Psalm 119:1-11).

Your daily input of God's Word might be in the form of Bible readings on tape. This is especially valuable for those with poor eyesight or for those who spend hours on the road. God's Word will begin a transforming work in our lives as we ingest daily doses into our spiritual systems.

Prayer

There is nothing like a specific, timely answer to prayer to cause our faith to soar! Sometimes we rebel and recoil if things are not going our way—needs that seem to remain unmet; enduring frustrating, unresolved conflict; or when pressure and calamity threaten to undo us. But it is through these very instances that God may become the most real to us.

Some of us turn to God only as a last resort. We face a desperate situation and have no remaining alternatives—then we beg God for the help we should have sought at the outset.

Prayer is vital in our communication with our heavenly Father. It can be a constant conversation or an intense interchange. It can be a comforting communion or an invigorating intercession. Prayer can become as natural as breathing or as labored as giving birth. Just as there is variety in the seasons of the year, so too, is there variety in the seasons of prayer. Each has its place; each has its rewards.

But we must not simply ponder prayer—we must pray; we must not just imagine interceding for a friend—we must intercede; we must not just contemplate communion—we must commune.

As a result of prayer, God will provide the power for us to do His will. "The prayer of a righteous man is powerful and effective" (James 5:16). I remember the early days of our marriage when Dave was going to school during the day while I stayed home with our daughter. Then in the evenings I would attend classes while he studied and entered into the life of our one-year-old.

It used to bother me greatly that I seemed to get nothing out of my personal time with the Lord. I would read and receive instruction, to be sure. I would pray and see answers to prayer, of course. But there seemed to be a vitality and power and meaning lacking in those times. I remember thinking, *Here we are in Bible school and I am struggling with dead devotions.*

A few years later, I went through many months of personal crisis that forced me to throw myself solely upon the mercy of almighty

God. It was a desperate dependency on His grace and wisdom, strength and power, compassion and love, that brought me through a potentially devastating time. It seemed that through those difficult months I spent more time on my knees than on my feet.

But I came to the end of it with a new appreciation of the Lord, His faithfulness, and the victory that is ours through Jesus Christ (1 Corinthians 15:57). No longer do times of Bible reading and prayer seem trite. No longer are requests uttered in apathy or vain repetitions. No longer is it a chore to cast my every care on Him (1 Peter 5:7).

Now it is a delight to enter into God's presence. There I find the pulse that beats to give my life power and purpose and the ever-abiding presence that can be trusted as my best friend. Now I draw upon God's wisdom to give direction moment by moment. Now I enjoy the fruits of the Spirit day by day. Now is a glimpse of what it will be like *then*.

Sometimes, though, we use prayer as a crutch to detain us from action. It may be easier to spend time on our knees than to get up and do what God is urging us to do. For instance, I would much prefer to spend time praying about writing this chapter than disciplining myself to finish it. For some reason, it has been an especially difficult one to write. Major interruptions, lack of motivation and energy, and frustration in condensing a vast subject into a few thousand words, have all plagued me since I began this chapter. Yes, I would much rather pray about it than do it!

It is interesting that Peter tells us, "The end of all things is near. Therefore be clear minded and self-controlled so that you can pray" (1 Peter 4:7). We usually think of it the other way around—we pray so that we can be self-controlled. We forget that it often takes discipline to do what God requires.

There are those who excel in discipline—the Olympian who trains every muscle of his body; the handicapped who persevere amid darkness, silence, pain, and helplessness; or the young mother who has to keep going, going, going. But hear the Word of the Lord:

Do you not know that in a race all the runners run, but only one gets the prize? Run in such a way as to get the prize. Everyone who competes in the games goes into strict training. They do it to get a crown that will not last; but we do it to get a crown that will last forever. Therefore I do not run like a man running aimlessly; I do not fight like a man beating the air. No, I beat my body and make it my slave so that after I have preached to others, I myself will not be disqualified for the prize. (1 Corinthians 9:24–27)

When you discipline yourself to pray, you are training yourself for that heavenly prize.

Evangelism

My introduction to evangelism came as a young Christian. I still remember clearly the joy in leading a child to the Lord. I walked on air for days to realize that another had been born again into the kingdom of God because of my witness.

Several months later I asked a respected Bible teacher about evangelism. Maybe I misinterpreted his answer, but this is what I thought he said: "Yes, you must take every opportunity to witness — with everyone you meet, everyone you talk to during the day, everyone you come in contact with."

This concept of evangelism causes undue guilt, forced sharing, offended hearers, and maybe even works *against* bringing someone to the Lord. There is a proper time and way to share our faith. To barge into someone's life uninvited may have its place, but more often than not, there may be a better way.

It's called lifestyle evangelism — allowing God to use the unique you to reach others, not by force or coercion but by a life of love reaching out to pull them in. It's recognizing that our day-to-day relationships offer opportunities to share the difference Jesus Christ has made in our lives.

We can share how Jesus Christ has given us freedom from guilt, loneliness, purposelessness, and eternal death. He has provided the way for us to have an abundant, joyful life, both now and in eternity. We need to become involved in other people's lives to the extent that they can see God's love for them through us.

Some have the gift of evangelism, of drawing the great numbers into the fold. There is a place for mass evangelism. There is also a place for one-on-one evangelism and discipling—walking with another in the Christian life to help him grow and mature in spiritual things.

God uses most of us through the working out of His plan in our lives; through our obedience to His leading; through willingly saying yes when He provides the opportunities to share. I wonder how many of the people I "led to the Lord" under duress are still faithful to Him? I wonder if my life has not had more impact on those with whom a friendship had first been built. I wonder if more people are not brought to the Lord as a result of my being faithful to His plan for my life than trying to follow the plans someone else says I should have.

This does not negate my responsibility in following that plan, and if it includes knocking on doors or preaching to the untold millions, then I *must* do it. If it means leading a home Bible study or starting an inner city mission, then I *will* obey. If it means handing out tracts to passers-by or hosting a children's Bible club, then I *choose* to respond. If it means visiting hospital rooms or holding services in nursing homes, then I *should* get involved. If it means befriending the unlovely, helping the hurting, or encouraging the downcast, then I *accept* it as my lot in life.

Whatever the calling, I will be faithful. I can do no less. I cannot be faithful to someone else's calling. We give ourselves untold grief when we compare our ministry with another's. If we are sincerely following the leading of God's Spirit and acting in obedience, then the issue of evangelism will be a joy, not a job; it will be a delight, not a dread; and it will be a pleasure, not a problem.

Summary

Our spiritual growth often follows a natural timetable. We cannot manufacture maturity; we can only cooperate with God as the Holy Spirit prompts us to follow His leading.

Proverbs 25:28 underscores the importance of self-control: "Like a city whose walls are broken down is a man who lacks self-control." Without the protection of self-control we open ourselves to all kinds of enemy attack. Self-control is important in gaining the athletic prize (1 Corinthians 9:25); it is an attribute of an elder

(Titus 1:8); and it is encouraged as a quality to be added to our faith (2 Peter 1:5-8).

Margie Anders, wife of Dr. Max Anders, says it well, "Get over the past, get order in the present, give others hope for the future."

Chapter Challenge

Begin with the first challenge and work for thirty minutes. If you finish sooner, continue with the other challenges. Pick up the next day where you left off and spend thirty minutes proceeding through the list until each item has been completed.

1. Is your life set apart for God's glory? Determine in your heart that you want to develop spiritual discipline.

2. Spend fifteen minutes a day for the next month reading the Word of God. After a month evaluate the difference it has made.

3. What does prayer mean to you? Spend time every day this week appreciating God for who He is, confessing your sins to Him, thanking God for all that He has done for you, and bringing your needs and hurts before Him.

4. Is God using you right now in a ministry of evangelism or discipling? Ask the Lord to give you a godly burden for someone, the opportunities to be a witness to that person, and the wisdom to know when to share and when to keep silent.

5. Are you being faithful to the calling that God has given you? If not, what steps do you need to take in order to be obedient?

PART THREE

CULTIVATING ONGOING SELF-DISCIPLINE

THE THRUST OF PERSONAL MOTIVATION

Scott was an optimistic dreamer. He had a pleasant outlook on life, and most people seemed to enjoy being with him. He had all kinds of plans for the future. The way Scott talked made you want to get in line behind the Pied Piper and march off to a wonderful life.

But few of Scott's dreams and possibilities actually came to fruition. His ideas stopped at the planning stage, and his dreams never made it beyond his thoughts. Somewhere he lost the connection between thinking and doing.

As a result, Scott eventually became frustrated and disappointed in himself. Pretty soon he stopped dreaming to avoid further discouragement. He seemed to blend into life with no real distinction and was swept along with the tide of humanity — never really living beyond his self-made fog.

What kept Scott from realizing his wonderful dreams? What could have spurred him to become all that God wanted him to be?

It was motivation. Motivation keeps us going when all seems futile. It gives sustenance to the word *perseverance*. It creates within us the desire to prevail no matter what the odds and inspires us to realms we never before entered. And it gives us reason to stretch when the easy thing would be to wither and die.

What Is Motivation?

Just what is motivation? Motivation produces an incentive within us to think, feel, or act in a certain way. It stimulates us to reach those goals we have never had the courage to voice. It is an inner impulse that prompts us toward either acceptable or unacceptable behavior, toward proper or improper thinking, toward rational or irrational emotions.

We are not always conscious of what motivates us. Perhaps we never realize outwardly what led us to embrace a particular behavior or set of values. Nevertheless, our motives play a vital role in who we are and who we will become.

Motive Versus Motivation

Motivation differs from motive. While a motive concerns a heart condition—the *why* of what we do—motivation deals with the practical manifestation of that motive. For instance, a young husband's motive for going to work each day may be to provide for the family he loves. His motivation may lie in the stack of bills in the desk drawer. A wife's motive in maintaining a clean house may be a desire for praise from her neighbors, while her motivation may be promising herself a reward when the cleaning is completed. Since our motivations stem originally from underlying motives, we will examine motivation in the hope of identifying underlying motives in the process.

Michael knew his life was going nowhere. In fact, people told him so all the time. He was a Casanova and had an aversion to work. Life to him was one big tilt-a-whirl with the vices of the world pulling and spinning his mind into chaos. But late one night, while in a drunken stupor, he meshed with the twisted metal of his car when he smashed into an electric pole.

Weeks in the hospital afforded him time to contemplate and reflect on the uselessness of his life. His motive for his behavior had always been to experience pleasure—trying to grasp all that the world says you can have. Funny thing, though, he never did find real pleasure. Oh, sure, what he did masqueraded as pleasure, but it was empty and void of any true satisfaction. What he needed, he came to see, was a purpose for living beyond himself.

During his hospital stay a local pastor visited Michael and showed him that, through giving his life to Jesus Christ, he would find the meaning and fulfillment he was looking for. It was not easy for Michael to turn his selfish and prideful ways over to the Lord, but he couldn't run any longer from the emptiness and despair that were ready to consume him. So, by faith, he reached out to Jesus Christ, asked His forgiveness for the sins that drove Christ to a cruel death on Michael's behalf, and asked Him to become Lord of his life.

From that day, Michael's attitude and behavior began to change. Sure, he still faced some of the same struggles, but his motives had changed. Now Michael wanted only to please the Lord, not himself. Now he wanted to pursue righteousness, not wickedness. Now he wanted to help others, not hinder them.

Because Michael's motive was pure, his life started to match up with that motive. The changes came slowly but steadily as year after year he worked out God's plan for his life. Changing his motive for living made all the difference for Michael.

Michael's motivation came in the form of the satisfaction he received from living a godly life and from encouraging many others whose situations were even more desperate than his had been. Michael was motivated by the warmth of love from fellow believers, from belonging to a church family that upheld and cared for one another, and by the contentment of knowing that God was molding him to become more like Jesus Christ.

Motivators

Our motivators can come in many forms. We go to great lengths to meet our needs, whether they be physiological (food, clothing, shelter), social acceptance, goal oriented, people oriented, a feeling of accomplishment, or obedience to God.

Social Acceptance. Nancy's tremendous need for social acceptance determined whether she felt exultant or downcast. Through social acceptance she found her worth or felt her lack of it. For it she gave up her identity, sacrificed her values, and desecrated that which had once been so precious. And in the end, she was left devastated and ruined — unacceptable both to herself and others.

Nancy's need, though not wrong in itself, motivated her to behave in extremes. The greater the need, the greater the motivation to have that need met. In Nancy's case it was met in ungodly ways. We all have God-given needs that can be met in honorable ways. Ours is the choice to pervert or purify.

Goals. Beyond that, our goals also motivate us to action. Knowing that what we do today will affect our tomorrows should cause us to consider if taking the easy way out is really worth it. Will it keep us from attaining what our hearts tell us is right for us? Will it hinder our long-term purpose? Even small choices will have some bearing on how quickly and in what manner we reach our goals.

Perhaps this is a good time to use a personal illustration. One of my future goals is athletic competition. I believe that as a result of taking care of my body and living according to God's principles, I am healthier today at forty than I was at twenty. That is the message I would like to proclaim through the channel of athletics. Now, I don't necessarily have any overwhelming desire to compete. In fact, it sort of scares me because it will be a new experience. My motive is to follow the plans I feel God has for my life.

But that doesn't mean I do nothing to prepare and train for the competition. Circumstances seem to assault my training programs every several months, and I start all over time and time again. Because much of my previous training involved an outdoor pool, weather has played a big role in keeping me from training consistently. Finally, in frustration, I decided to make the mini-tramp a key ingredient of my current program.

So, a few months ago I started jogging one minute on the mini-tramp three times a day. When I reached my current level of sixty minutes three times a day, I began to increase the intensity instead of the amount of time. (While building up time I often ended the session in a slow shuffle rather than a jubilant jog. My only criteria was to keep moving.)

I have several motivations for getting up at 3:45 in the morning and jogging until 7:15 five days a week (allowing for stretching time), but the most compelling is that I haven't missed a quota since I started this particular program. A little chart in my notebook would have a blank square if I decided to skip my morning jaunt.

Sticking to something motivates me greatly. The same concept is true in not having eaten desserts in three years. I certainly am not going to break my record now with that chocolate eclair or piece of pecan pie!

Understandably, my guidelines are self-imposed, and my husband sometimes says, "You're nuts!" But I have lived both ways and for me, life is far more fulfilling and actually grants greater freedom when I have a rein on personal discipline.

Another motivator is what I accomplish during my three hours on the mini-tramp. I read, listen to tapes, memorize Scripture, go over my prayer list, sort out my schedule, lift weights (amateur style), and even edit manuscripts. The time is constructive in its own right, and I get fit simultaneously!

During the building-up phase of this program, I would ask myself, "Why am I doing this dumb thing? I should be in bed, or at least doing something more sane." Then I would remind myself of the underlying motive for doing it in the first place — that of allowing the Lord to fulfill His plan in my life. And at this point, I feel that plan will include competition.

At the very least, if the competition does not materialize, I know I am more in shape because of the training. Who knows? Disease or some other debilitating factor may cause me to abandon the program. But until then, with the motive comes a commitment to reach a future goal.

People. People also motivate us. We respond and are moved out of love to do that which is unpleasant or difficult. History resounds with instances of love motivating people to acts of devotion and sacrifice. The supreme sacrifice because of love was Jesus Christ's death on the cross for us.

Let me tell you about a young, very attractive, engaged couple I know. Brad and Sharon have magnetizing influence for righteousness on young people. It is not something manufactured or pretended. It is real and contagious. It shouts in untold ways, "I care about you! God cares about you! Live your life to the full by living in submission to Him!"

Sharon has excelled over the years in gymnastics. Through her example and love for the other gymnasts, she has made an impact on their lives far beyond what she realizes. Whether it be encouraging the girls to live a godly life, or by being an exciting role model in her relationship with Brad, Sharon has caused the girls to thirst for righteousness in their own lives. She has given them the motivation to reach beyond the mediocre and teenage norm. Because of her life, others have been enriched, blessed and spurred onto excellence in their Christian walk. Though their paths may never cross again, the girls will always remember the love Sharon had for them, the high standards of a godly calling, and the inspiration to become all that they could be through Jesus Christ.

And Brad's mesmerizing effect on youth for godliness has literally snatched some from the clutches of death. One mother called to thank Brad for the influence he had on her son who was at the brink of suicide. She shared that because of Brad and who he was, her son decided against taking his own life. When Brad asked her son's name, it was someone he didn't even know.

Then there are those he does know, and invests his time, his love, and his life in helping. Most recently was the young man named Rick who was headed down a thorny patch, sure to end in destruction, had not the Lord intervened through Brad.

Rick had tuned out all authority figures, but came to trust Brad as a friend although he was six years his elder. Brad's love gripped Rick's heart. The way Brad's eyes bore into Rick's very soul; the tenderness with which Brad assured Rick of his care and concern; the hours spent listening and encouraging; the sacrifice of a major career investment the night Brad spent searching for Rick when his whereabouts were unknown — all proved the depth of Christ's love in Brad's heart for the hurting.

As a result, Rick made a complete turnaround. Brad was someone who finally believed in him for who he was. Someone who would not let him go despite the ugliness that Brad must see. Someone who desired God's best for him and would help him achieve it no matter what the cost. Here was love demonstrated, love motivated, love personified—the embodiment of the characteristics of Jesus Christ that we are all called to embrace.

Young people would say that Brad and Sharon offered friendship as a gift to cherish. The following poem says it well . . .

The Essence of Friendship
(Used by Permission)

Friends are those who feel with me the joys and sorrows, the longings and desires, the hopes and dreams, the cares and burdens.

They can share and feel. They are there to share my silence or my lofty thoughts. They are there to comfort when I hurt, to inspire when I despair, to encourage when I'm discouraged, to hope when all seems hopeless.

They are there to feel with me the disappointments and dejections as well as the thrills and excitements.

They laugh with me and we have a unique bond of mutual merriment. They notice the little things that bring me joy . . . flowers, sunsets, warm breezes, birds' melodies, deep thoughts, kindnesses, music, and innocent children.

They are not afraid to be alone with me. Alone in silent thought, but together, sharing the silence.

They desire for me strength of character and depth of insight. They can cry with me and understand the meaning of my tears.

They are ready to give of themselves until life itself would be offered as a gift.

My friends cause me to reach for that unreachable star because they believe in me. And for them I reach; higher than I ever thought possible.

They make me want to be my best self, to believe in myself. In them I find that part of myself that I always wanted to be.

They bring out the highest of virtues, because they focus only on the virtues. Though there is much that is unseemly, they pass over and encourage only the good.

My friends see me as radiant and therefore I feel radiant. They see beauty, creating its own form of beauty in me. They multiply my happiness and divide my sadness.

When no one else cares, they stand beside me; pulling for me, and ever, ever believing in me. And yet, they don't stifle me, but give me room to grow and sometimes fail.

Why?

Because they love me. In their own way they love me. My friends.

May I in turn be a friend to them. With all that the word encompasses.

Then we will all know the meaning of friendship. . . . having experienced it for ourselves, glorying in it, and cherishing that bond we have with one another.

And you Brad and Sharon . . . you are my friends!

Feeling of Accomplishment. What we need to do is determine what motivates us personally and then capitalize on that motivator to move ahead, provided both the motive and motivator are pure. For some people restoring order or gaining a sense of completeness ranks high on the list of motivators. This is also a big one for me.

Visualizing a project completed encourages me to keep going when I would rather call it quits. This is especially true beyond the halfway mark. I feel a great sense of satisfaction when I can orchestrate the completion of a large project.

I remember thinking one day after I had thoroughly cleaned the house (for me a clean house is one where every drawer is straightened, the ironing and laundry are caught up, the fridge is clean, and the woodwork is washed) that it must have felt something like this for the Lord when He finished creation—that it was complete and He could pronounce His work good.

Let's not forget a modern-day motivator—deadlines. Meeting a deadline produces a great feeling of accomplishment. But some people are motivated only by deadlines. Make deadlines work for you but don't become a slave to them. Always allow for some slack if things don't go as planned—because they usually don't.

Obedience to God. Our desires motivate us to pursue either good or evil. That's why it is critical to identify our desires, make sure they are godly, and then work out a plan of action to fulfill them (which may include waiting for the Lord's timing).

Obedience to God is the ultimate motivator when everything in us screams for an easier way. James encourages us that perseverance works in us so that we may be mature and complete, not lacking anything (see James 1:4).

And Peter tells us that there is a reason for perseverance and self-control:

> His divine power has given us everything we need for life and godliness through our knowledge of him who called us by his own glory and goodness. Through these he has given us his very great and precious promises, so that through them you may participate in the divine nature and escape the corruption in the world caused by evil desires.

> For this very reason, make every effort to add to your faith goodness; and to goodness, knowledge; and to knowledge, self-control; and to self-control, perseverance; and to perseverance, godliness; and to godliness, brotherly kindness; and to brotherly kindness, love. For if you possess these qualities in increasing measure, they will keep you from being ineffective and unproductive in your knowledge of our Lord Jesus Christ. (2 Peter 1:3-8)

Motivational Styles

Our basic temperament can be a factor in determining what motivates us. Some people are motivated by achievements. They work well alone, thrive on lists, and are not thwarted by a lack of praise from others. These people's lives can be summarized by the word *do*.

Other people are motivated by the ability to influence others. They lead and manage others well, like to be recognized for their leadership abilities, and need the freedom to do things their own way. Their lives can be summarized by the word *control*.

Still others are motivated by their social affiliations. They need friends and thrive in groups. Their lives can be summarized by the words *acceptance* and *approval*.

Each of us probably has a dominant motivational style. If we learn to appreciate the characteristics of each style, we will come to a greater understanding of others and be able to encourage them by focusing on their particular motivators.

Increasing Your Personal Motivation

At the risk of oversimplifying the subject, the following are some steps you can take to increase your personal motivation.

- List the benefits of the change you are contemplating, or from completing a certain task.
- List the problems that will result if you do not follow through.
- Observe others who have failed to follow through in the same area and ask yourself if you want to be like them.
- Find out what God's Word says about the situation.
- Allow the Holy Spirit to convict and teach you.
- Make sure your priorities are clear in your mind.
- Eliminate all that is clogging the channels which might keep you from following through. (You can't get up early because you watch the late movie. You can't spend time with your children because you get together with the boys every day after work.)
- Help someone else accomplish what you are trying to do.
- Clear away the crutches that have been keeping you from doing what you know you should do. (Allowing your husband to drive you places because you are in a new town and you have a fear of getting lost.)
- Increase your belief and enthusiasm for what God can do in your life.

Julie's Story

Originally I had intended to use Julie's story as an illustration in the chapter on physical self-discipline. But after our interview I realized that what she had to say went beyond mere physical limitation and delved into the core of her daily existence — the motivation to make it through one more day.

The first time I saw Julie I was swimming laps at the health club. She was a walking skeleton and looked old and haggard. But there was also something young and fresh about her. I have since learned that she is in her early forties, and the freshness is from her relationship with the Lord, her outlook on life, and her love for her family.

Sixteen years ago Julie developed a muscle disease which has affected every part of her body. From the assimilation, digestion, and elimination of food to carrying out simple tasks, Julie has had to train her muscles to work for her. She must concentrate on the muscles that help her swallow, on the muscles that help her breathe, and on the muscles that help her walk. The doctor's prognosis is that she will spend her future in a wheel chair.

It was chilly the day I went to interview Julie. She was exercising in a hot tub when I arrived. For my benefit we went inside where it was warmer. During the brief time I visited with Julie, her bony feet and legs began to turn blue.

She must exercise her muscles constantly to aid her circulation. At times she has to exercise and perform physical therapy techniques up to eighteen hours a day. It is a slow, tedious process, and those who could not exhibit discipline in the extreme would soon be annihilated through severe atrophy of the muscles.

As a child Julie was a competitive ice skater and excelled in academics as well. It has always been important for Julie to do her best to please her parents and have someone say, "I'm proud of you."

Today that same desire motivates Julie to do her best. Only now it's not achieving high grades or winning an athletic competition — it's getting out of bed in the morning and refusing to give in to the constant pain and weakness. It's focusing on having a positive attitude and being thankful for even being alive. It's wanting to give to others from a depleted storehouse of energy in spite of the personal sacrifice it involves. And it's learning day by day that God is sovereign and agreeing to be submissive to that sovereignty.

It is still important for Julie to hear someone say, "I'm proud of you." Only now it might be from her husband — "Honey, I'm proud of you for making it through the day." Or from her doctors — "Julie,

I'm proud of you for doing your exercises." Or from her children —
"Mom, we're proud of you for being able to still laugh."

Julie has learned to make the best of each day. She usually
selects one reason why it is important for her to keep going. The
day of the interview it was the anticipation of my visit. It may be
fixing chili, her husband's favorite dish, for dinner. On Valentine's
Day she told herself, "I've got to feel good today because someone
might send me flowers and I want to have enough energy to show
my excitement."

Routine helps Julie persevere. She doesn't have to think about
what comes next. Her morning routine includes exercising on a sta-
tionery bike, therapy in the hot tub, and perhaps a little walking. In
the afternoon routine she makes lunch, struggles to eat it, and then
exercises again in the hot tub. Routine offers structure and encouragement to Julie's day. She knows that if she made it through yesterday's routine, she can make it through today's as well.

Another motivational factor for Julie is the severe consequences
she will experience if she tries to take the easy way out. For instance, she may prefer to go to bed after lunch as an escape from
the pain instead of doing her exercises, but she has learned that it is
not worth it. The stiffness and pain simply magnify and are far
worse than before.

Julie says she has the most wonderful, understanding husband
in the world. While I was there he called to see how she was doing
because she had had a difficult morning. They have shed many
tears together when it looked as if Julie was too weak to continue
the fight. But he is ever at her side, ever sacrificing and loving and
caring. It is because of him and for him that many days she refuses
to give up when those with less determination have done just that.

And then there is her relationship with the Lord. She has a
diary where she records, only for Him, her times of questioning,
times of praising, and times of suffering. She is confident that He is
ever with her, giving her the strength to hang on when it would be
easier to despair. And it is her love for the Lord that causes her to
want to use this experience to encourage someone else in their pain,
in their questioning, and in their hopelessness.

Julie exhorts people to not always be so serious about life. Enjoy
something about every day. Think young and you can feel young,

whether or not your body agrees. Dare to dream in spite of your limitations. Julie has dreams. She would like to go to school to be a nurse or follow her father's footsteps of being a florist. But above all, Julie wants to love people and inspire them to become all that they can be in whatever situation they find themselves.

Summary

Change usually cannot come without motivation. It may be internal or external pressure that produces the incentive to act. It may be that we have reached the point of absorption of an irritant and we will not rest until the irritant is removed or our attitude toward it is changed.

It is to our advantage to identify what motivates us and capitalize on it for our good. Determine what is important to you and focus on it while trying to induce a change in your life.

Our goal in change is progress, not perfection. Perseverance is born out of hope. Do you hope or fear the future? Hope is a great motivator, on both a small and large scale. You talk yourself into going to the mailbox when you don't feel like it because you hope there will be a special letter for you. You stick to your diet because you hope one day it will pay off.

We have an eternal hope that does not disappoint, that motivates us toward excellence in every area of our lives, and that gives us a reason for being and a purpose for living that none can take away.

Chapter Challenge

Begin with the first challenge and work for thirty minutes. If you finish sooner, continue with the other challenges. Pick up the next day where you left off and spend thirty minutes proceeding through the list until each item has been completed.

1. List ten things that motivate you personally — praise from a boss, the satisfaction of a job well done, a goal accomplished, happiness you bring to another.
2. Think about several instances when you were highly motivated. What was the motivating factor in each case?

3. Make contact with someone you admire who is motivated in the area in which you wish to become more disciplined. Discover their secrets of success.

4. Do something tangible that you were inspired to do as a result of reading this chapter.

ADJUSTING EXPECTATIONS TO REALITY

M el hated doing taxes. Every year the project loomed over him from January until August. (Because he waited so long, he usually would have to apply for an extension.) His paperwork was a mess. He just threw his receipts into a big box along with piles of other paperwork.

Each year his taxes seemed to get more and more complicated. Even though he had an accountant prepare his returns, he still had to get all the paperwork together for the accountant. Sometimes it would take him weeks just to push himself to look through the pile of debris he called paperwork.

Mel dreaded taxes. But no matter how long Mel put off doing them, they were still there. It was getting so that every year around January Mel became impossible to live with for six months. He felt the heavy stress constantly and couldn't relax. Life for Mel was miserable. Oh, how he hated taxes!

Then there was Christine. Christine disliked doing laundry so much that her family often had to dig out socks from the dirty clothes before school. And her husband's clothes looked rumpled because she hated ironing. Christine herself looked as if she just missed the mark, although her clothes were nice enough.

The laundry in Christine's home was a continual source of irritation for the whole family. If only she could do away with laundry, her life would be much happier!

What do Mel and Christine have in common? They both have developed habits of procrastination. Procrastination is putting off what we *should* do in exchange for a more pleasurable, easier, or more understandable activity. Procrastination is not merely postponing something because you don't have the time; it is *avoiding* doing something even if time is not the issue.

Roots of Procrastination

There are many causes of procrastination, to be sure, but we will touch on only the major ones. Perhaps you will be able to trace your own route to developing procrastination and then find help for overcoming the habits that have become so ingrained.

First of all, think back to your childhood or teen-age years. Can you remember your first incidence of procrastination? Is there a specific time when you *chose* purposely not to do something when you knew you should? Maybe it was the paper you needed to write for school. It seemed like an overwhelming task, and you didn't really understand it anyway, so you just kept pretending it wasn't there.

Or maybe it was doing the dishes. If you did the dishes right away after supper and did a good job, your mother was so pleased that she had you do another job as well. But if you dawdled, she didn't bother because you had worked long enough.

Or perhaps you felt your parents had too much control over you when you were a teen-ager. Instead of rebelling outright, you took forever doing the things you knew they wanted you to do.

Fear of Failure. Some people procrastinate because they are afraid of failing. They reason, "If I never get around to doing this or that, then nobody (including myself) will ever see me fail." The fallacy of that kind of thinking is that by putting something off, we in essence are failing nonetheless, although not as blatantly. At the root of a fear of failure is often poor self-esteem—how you *feel* about yourself—reflected through fear.

Shawna enjoyed writing and seemed to have a natural gift for creating stories. When she was a teen-ager, her mother noticed her talent and urged her to send one of her stories to a magazine for publication. Shawna was thrilled with the idea and eagerly waited for the mail every day.

When she saw her return envelope, she tore it open expecting to find her first check from her writing. She was devastated when the envelope revealed only a form rejection slip. From then on, she just dabbled at her writing, never being able to bring herself to finish a story.

Amid her mother's urging and nagging about Shawna not living up to her potential, Shawna kept repressing the desire to write. She was so afraid of failing again! If she never sent another story to a magazine, she would never have to feel that sense of rejection again. Instead of using her failure to motivate her, Shawna let it destroy a valuable gift.

Fear of Success. Others procrastinate because of a fear of success. They reason, "I succeeded that time, but it was probably just luck. I'll never be able to do it again. Besides, if I do succeed again, I will have to *keep on* succeeding and I don't really want to." Or, "If I am a success, then other people won't like me or be comfortable around me. I would rather have love than success."

Phillip loved his job as an advertising account executive. He especially enjoyed coming up with creative campaign ideas. One of his ideas caught on so big in a national campaign that he was offered a promotion, his name began appearing in newspapers around the country, and people started treating him with awe.

The success was so overpowering that Phillip began having anxiety attacks whenever he tried to work on future campaigns. "What if I can't come up with another good idea? And, if I do, what if I can't keep it up?" He also decided subconsciously that he would rather have people be his friends than hold him in awe at arm's length.

So Phillip started missing deadlines, turned in poor marketing plans, and lost the zing in his promotions. He was trying to recapture the way it was before his success.

Desire to Control. A third reason some people procrastinate is be-cause they use it as a weapon in gaining control, albeit a subser-vient control. Nadine was an efficient secretary, always on top of things, always done with her work ahead of schedule. When her boss noticed that Nadine seemed to have extra time on her hands toward the end of the day, he began to find things for her to do — busy work — because it bothered him to pay someone if they were not going top speed all day long.

Nadine resented how her boss would dump a new project on her just when she was finishing the day's work. And she could see that the projects were often meaningless time wasters. "How dare he treat me as if I am not using my time efficiently! I'll show him!"

Nadine began to purposely take longer on her daily tasks so that by the end of the afternoon she would still have things to do. In fact, she even began to make her boss wait for that report or the letter he wanted in the mail yesterday. Sure, he could fire her, but she knew she could easily get another job, so that didn't worry her. Maybe her boss would apologize for his petty tactics and then they could resume business as normal. Two could play this game!

Self-Protection. Procrastination is often a means of self-protection. Can you determine what is the root of your procrastination? There may be different reasons for various circumstances. It might be as simple as not wanting to put forth the effort of completing a project because you have developed a habit of doing what you want, when you want. You may feel the effort expended is not going to be worth the eventual reward, so why bother?

You may have gotten by all these years with someone else bail-ing you out — your parents because of a false concept of love, your teachers because you were the star football player, your boss be-cause your dad was a prominent community member, your secre-tary because she had a crush on you, your wife because she felt it was her duty . . . and on it goes.

But, one day you *will* have to face your responsibility no matter how unlikely that seems now. Far better to learn to do what you should (but don't *feel* like doing) now than in a situation where you really care about the outcome.

Think again. Are you procrastinating to get attention, to hold on to someone you love by having them always take care of you, or even the opposite — to keep someone from desiring you if you allowed yourself to be the person you know you *could* be?

Maybe you patterned your life after a procrastinating parent, you don't have the energy to do what you know you should, or perhaps you fear criticism even if you do your best. Maybe you just plain don't *know* how to do a particular task so you keep putting it off, only to face the grave consequences later.

Overcoming Habits of Procrastination

You first need to determine in which areas you procrastinate regularly. Is it in household chores, paperwork, areas of conflict with family members, financial matters, developing close relationships, or taking vacations?

Then, analyze why you are procrastinating in that area. For example, perhaps you have been avoiding taking care of your correspondence. It has been piling up all year. Your desk is such a mess that you're not sure what is what. Besides, you hate to write letters anyway!

But it has been gnawing at you for months. And the bills. You hate paying bills so you just stash them until you get final notices. Then you pay them and hope the check doesn't bounce, since you haven't balanced the checkbook for months.

Here is how I would approach the problem. First of all, set aside an hour when you can begin to go through the pile on your desk. Set the timer if you want. Sit on the floor with the biggest stack in front of you.

Now, as you pick up the top piece of paper decide if it is:

- a letter to be answered;
- a bill to be paid;
- something that should be kept and therefore filed;
- something you want to read sometime;
- something that can be tossed.

As you go through each piece of paper put it into a corresponding pile. At the end of the hour you should have five piles. It would be helpful to have five baskets or small boxes to keep the papers in until you can get to them another time.

Keep setting aside an hour here and there until there are no more stacks of paperwork on your desk. Then, open a new bank account, if necessary, to start out fresh, allowing the old account to be phased out. Make it a habit to balance your checkbook every month. Ask someone to show you if you are not sure how to do it.

Pay the bills that must be paid first and have an incoming bill box. Set up a system so you know what bills are due when each month. If you get paid twice a month, determine what bills will come out of the first check every month and which out of the second. Then, make it a habit to pay them the day after you get your check.

Next, tackle your correspondence by writing out a master letter to a friend. Determine to write one or two letters a day, using the master letter as a guide, until you are all caught up. I prefer to set aside one day a month to catch up on all my correspondence. Then I can forget about it for a month without feeling like it is continually hanging over my head.

As paperwork comes in, take care of it immediately, at least to the point of putting it into one of the five piles. Train yourself not to just toss it into the center of the desk on top of yesterday's mail. Either set aside a few minutes each day to take care of it, or do it immediately as you receive it, whether it be the mail or kid's school papers.

Relating specifically to the correspondence, ask yourself if there is some other reason why you don't want to answer it—you don't like some of the people that write to you, you don't feel it is worth the time to write to others, you can't formulate your thoughts, you have nothing to say, or you hate the thought of having to do it.

Some alternatives might be:

- Just answer other people's letters with postcards—at least they know you are thinking of them.
- Send form letters run off on a copy machine—it's better than nothing.
- Hire a word processing service to do your letters for you—it may cost more but it may be worth it.

- Send a printed letter saying you will answer personal correspondence in the future, but due to time commitments you are keeping in touch this way for now. At least people will not keep writing you and being resentful that you don't write back.

Often we procrastinate because the task seems overwhelming. By breaking the project down into smaller components, not only do we make it more manageable, but we often can muster enough motivation to tackle part of a formidable task, whereas the whole would have threatened to undo us.

On paper, name the project and then list all of the steps you will need to take in order to complete it. Then, list the benefits of having the job done and the consequences of not having it done on time. Make note of the reasons why you don't want to complete it, or even to begin it. Meet these excuses head-on by finding a corresponding reason to invalidate the excuse.

Commit your work to the Lord. Set aside a day and time to begin. Before you leave the project, set up another time on your calendar to start the next step. Visualize the progress you want to make. And finally, reward yourself for completing each step. Make a game of it, taking time to appreciate the work you've done.

Once we have completed our think-outs (see chapter 2) we may find that many of the tasks that we have been procrastinating about may not be part of God's plan for us at all. Eliminating unnecessary tasks is the easiest way to combat procrastination. Being convinced that a task *is* in fact part of God's plan for us is the second easiest way to overcome procrastination by giving us the determination to forge ahead.

Perfectionism Exposed

Perfectionism is that driving need to approach any task with the idea that if it is not done perfectly then my self-worth suffers in some way. The desire for self-acceptance or other-acceptance is manifested through striving, striving, striving.

Now there is nothing wrong in striving to do our best. But there comes a point when striving for excellence becomes compulsive — when the underlying reason for the striving is to prove ourselves.

Our underlying motive for striving for excellence should be to bring glory to Jesus Christ through our obedience.

There is freedom in allowing Jesus Christ to motivate us. There is bondage in the compulsive need to prove our worth. Our worth has already been determined. In God's eye we are worth the ultimate sacrifice He could make — that of allowing His son to die on our behalf.

One's self-worth is often based on abilities and performance rather than on the value God sees in us. Perfectionism is one way to keep our lives in our control rather than turning them over to God's control. It's saying, "I can make it to heaven on my own terms."

Or, for the Christian, it's saying, "Sure, you paid a price for my life, now I'm going to show that I was worth the price." Perfectionists forget that no amount of attainment can buy or keep salvation. It is only through the grace of God, a gift given out of love, that we are offered salvation.

The devastating results of a life based on perfectionistic standards include frustration, anxiety, discouragement, a sense of helplessness, fear, and unrealistic stress. Since none of us is perfect, our striving is futile if we accept only perfection, whether in ourselves or others. There is a fine line between excellence and perfectionism. Excellence can be content with having tried to do our best. Perfectionism cannot.

Co-workers, friends, and acquaintances admired Lori as *the* woman of excellence. She always seemed to have everything under control. Everything she did, she did to perfection. Her house was immaculate, her children were well-dressed and well-mannered, her work at the office was done flawlessly, and her sacrificial involvement in church activities put others to shame. Such was the outward appearance of Lori's life.

However, if you could look at Lori's life behind the scenes, you might come to feel that yours wasn't so bad after all. Lori was literally driving herself to a nervous breakdown. She hounded her kids and husband lest her image of perfection be distorted in any way.

She was irritable with her family for not performing to her standards. Her kids felt as if they could never measure up. Walls were building and masks were forming. Behind the scenes, Lori complained profusely about her co-workers and fellow church members.

She pushed and pushed herself to do better, always fearful that she might find out the truth about herself—that she indeed was less than perfect, and therefore in her eyes, not acceptable.

If you find yourself with perfectionistic tendencies, you don't have to be resigned to their tyranny the rest of your life. You *can* change.

First, determine the cause of your poor self-image or the underlying motive for pushing yourself so hard. Are you trying to measure up to your parents' expectations of long ago? Are you trying to overcome guilt, either real of false? Or, are you trying to prove something to someone, maybe to get vengeance for a wrong committed? Roots of perfectionism can be very deep and painful. You may need to seek help from your pastor or from a qualified counselor.

Then, decide in your heart to do all that you do for the Lord Jesus Christ and His glory, realizing that He expects your best, *not* perfection. Be satisfied with your best. Also, listen to your self-talk when you tend to push yourself to compulsive limits. What are you saying? Replace your self-lies with the truth of the Word of God.

Reward yourself when you sense you are making progress. Share your struggles with a friend and learn to appreciate God's continual work in you.

Summary

The process of procrastination usually takes more effort than just getting up and doing what we have been putting off. If you struggle with procrastination, try the following steps:

1. Define what it is you are procrastinating about.
2. Do *something* toward starting the project. Look up the phone number, address an envelope, put the clothes for the dry cleaners by the door, collect your research material. Often the momentum will carry you through to begin the next step.
3. Catch yourself when you begin to make excuses and immediately commit your way to the Lord.
4. Avoid activity as a means of skirting the real project.
5. Do the worst part of the project first.
6. Reward yourself at every stage of completion.

Perfectionism differs from excellence in that perfection can never be attained — excellence can. Be mindful of those areas where your perfectionistic tendencies threaten to go beyond healthy excellence.

Chapter Challenge

Begin with the first challenge and work for thirty minutes. If you finish sooner, continue with the other challenges. Pick up the next day where you left off and spend thirty minutes proceeding through the list until each item has been completed.

1. Each of us procrastinates in some area of our lives. Select the one that is most aggravating to you and begin to work on it as outlined in the chapter.

2. Are you a perfectionist? This differs from trying to do a specific job with excellence and then being satisfied that we did our best. It is a pervasive attitude of struggling to do better, never being satisfied with your best. If this sounds like you, take the steps mentioned in the chapter to try to control your perfectionistic tendencies.

A FINAL WORD
OF ENCOURAGEMENT

Leon was fed up with his life. He seemed to be going nowhere, had little satisfaction in living, and was discontent with the person he had allowed himself to become. It was through a friend's life that Leon first received hope that things could be different.

Yes, he had given his life to Jesus Christ. Yes, he wanted to make a difference in the world. Yes, he knew that God had a specific plan for his life. But knowing these things and acting on them seemed to be poles apart. He was mesmerized by the mundane, squelched by stress, and discouraged by defeat.

Leon's friend, Bill, seemed to have something that commanded respect, achieved results, and made you glad you were his friend. Bill had stresses and defeats as did Leon, but he didn't let them keep him down for long. Bill shared with Leon that the missing ingredient in his life may be self-discipline — that quality of tenacity that is developed day by day through struggles, being dependent on the Holy Spirit for the strength to be faithful.

Over the course of several months Bill taught Leon many principles of self-discipline. What a change it made in Leon's life! No longer was he just jostling from one activity to another. No more would he condone commitments that were not God's best for him. Never again could he hoard harmful habits without knowing that God wanted something better for him.

But it was not easy. It took hard work, many failures, and much perseverance. Leon worked on one major change at a time until it became ingrained and automatic. With the supernatural help of the Holy Spirit, Leon found true success. He was faithful in using the resources and opportunities God had given him.

Something has also changed in Leon's closeness to the Lord. If Jesus were to come in person, Leon knows that his reaction would not be to hang back as a stranger as it would have been in the past. No, it would be more of a welcoming and embracing Him as a friend, and hugging Him as a father. That change in his relationship with Christ has made all the difference in motivating him to keep on becoming all that God wants him to become. Leon found that no other human being can completely understand or heal a broken heart. Only Jesus Christ can do that even though he often uses other people to meet our needs. For Leon, He sent Bill.

Bill helped Leon to regularly evaluate his progress. He showed him that small successes lead to major accomplishments. If Leon had quit, he would have only had the agony of the attempt, not the fulfillment of the finish. It was interesting that as Leon prepared himself in the areas that he felt God would have him pursue, opportunities soon opened to use those very skills. And it seemed the Lord gave him direction to choose only those best opportunities, and the best seemed to be staggered so that there was a continual supply with adequate breaks in between.

So often Leon found that if he stepped out in faith, God would give him the strength to keep him going. Leon knew that there would always be battles in life. But he was finding that through developing self-discipline in every area, more and more of those battles ended in victory instead of defeat. He had acquired a personal freedom that he had never felt before under the bondage of trying to do it his own way.

Leon had disciplined his spirit which led to a disciplined mind, body, and will for the glory of God.

An underlying motive for developing self-discipline in my life is not to go faster and faster, and accomplish more and more. But rather, it is to eliminate that which would hinder the pursuit of God's best for my life. It is to free me to have time for the most important activities — time with my family, time to spend an afternoon with a troubled friend, time to enjoy God's creation, and most of all, time with the Lord Himself.

One of the earliest lessons in self-discipline that I can remember happened when I was in junior high (I think). I was in the habit of watching television in the evenings. This one particular evening I had a great deal of homework and was torn between doing it or watching television. I remember going to my mother and saying, "Mom, why don't you just tell me I can't watch television tonight. Then it will be easier for me to do my homework."

My mother wisely replied, "No, you have to make those decisions for yourself. You will have to develop the discipline within yourself to do what you don't want to do." (This rendition is paraphrased, being filtered through years of fuzzy memories — but the gist is the same.)

Consider that in contrast to the tribute of my husband. Dione was complaining when it was her turn to vacuum and she didn't see why Mom shouldn't do it, "probably because she is just lazy." I heard Dave answer her, "Your mother is one of the most self-disciplined people I know." Yes, self-discipline *can* be learned.

And through working on these principles, you can learn self-discipline as well. It does not come naturally for me, and it probably won't for you either. It is not easy, but with God's help wouldn't you rather put forth a little more effort and be rewarded a hundredfold?

You don't have to buy a host of books covering each area of your life, looking for that one chapter on self-discipline. You have a blueprint in your hands to give you enough to get started. And then, for those areas that you particularly struggle with, select and study one or two books from the suggested reading list.

Review *Habits of the Heart* on an annual basis and see how far you've come in one year. As God orchestrates events in your life to bring about His best for you, cooperate with Him, step out in faith, and then trust Him for the strength to persevere. The depth of our character often determines the height of our success.

There is always the danger in writing a book of this nature of setting yourself up for a fall. Satan loves to discredit the name of

Christ. As you look to Jesus Christ as your example, don't allow the failures of others to keep you from becoming what you can be. We are all human, we are all frail as dust. Look only to Jesus, the author and finisher of our faith.

This book is an extension of my life. In it I have shared some intensely personal thoughts. And I do it in the hope you may be encouraged, inspired, and instructed. I am aware of the tendency of some, as the Pharisees in Jesus' day, to criticize, discredit, and judge. In fact, we are warned in Matthew 7:6 not to cast our pearls before swine lest they "trample them under their feet, and then turn and tear you to pieces."

Habits of the Heart is a part of my collection of pearls. If you have valid criticism or words of encouragement, I would love to hear from you in care of this publisher. May the God of all grace richly bless you with His best for your life as you seek to serve Him with all your heart, mind, and will.

BIBLIOGRAPHY

Suggested Reading for Part 1

Berry, Jo. *Managing Your Life and Time.* Zondervan, 1986.

Culp, Stephanie. *How to Get Organized When You Don't Have the Time.* Writer's Digest Books, 1986.

Davenport, Rita. *Making Time/Making Money.* St. Martin's Press, 1982.

Douglass, Merrill E. and Donna N. *Manage Your Time/Manage Your Work/Manage Yourself.* American Management Association, 1980.

Edwards, Judson. *Regaining Control of Your Life.* Bethany House, 1989.

Erickson, Kenneth A. *Christian Time Management.* Concordia, 1985.

Fronk, Ron L. *Creating a Lifestyle You Can Live With.* Whitaker House, 1988.

Suggested Reading for Part 2
Mental Self-Discipline:

Backus, William, and Chapian, Marie. *Telling Yourself the Truth.* Bethany House Publishers, 1980.

Collins, Gary R. *Your Magnificent Mind.* Baker Book House, 1980.

Gaughan, Harold. *Lord, Help Me Not to Have These Evil Thoughts.* Global Publishers, Inc., 1988.

LaHaye, Tim. *The Battle for the Mind.* Fleming H. Revell Co., 1980.

Minirth, Frank B., and Meier, Paul D. *Happiness Is a Choice.* Baker Book House, 1978.

Emotional Self-Discipline:

Carter, Les. *Mind Over Emotions.* Baker Book House, 1985.

Leman, Kevin, and Carlson, Randy. *Unlocking the Secrets of Your Childhood Memories.* Thomas Nelson Publishers, 1989.

Littauer, Fred and Florence. *Freeing Your Mind from Memories That Bind.* Here's Life Publishers, 1988.

Lutzer, Erwin. *Managing Your Emotions.* Victor Books, 1988.

Seamands, David. *Healing of Memories.* Victor Books, 1985.

Seamands, David A. *Healing for Damaged Emotions.* Victor Books, 1989.

Moral Self-Discipline:

Backus, William. *Finding the Freedom of Self-Control.* Bethany House Publishers, 1987.

Bussell, Harold L. *Lord, I Can Resist Anything but Temptation.* Zondervan Publishing House, 1985.

Dobson, James C. *Love Must Be Tough.* Word Books, 1983.

Dunn, Jerry G. *God Is for the Alcoholic.* Moody Press, 1975.

Lutzer, Erwin W. *How to Say No to a Stubborn Habit.* Victor Books, 1984.

Mowday, Lois. *The Snare.* NavPress, 1988.

Petersen, J. Allan. *The Myth of the Greener Grass.* Tyndale House Publishers, Inc., 1983.

Financial Self-Discipline:

Blue, Ron. *The Debt Squeeze.* Focus on the Family Publishing, 1989.

Blue, Ron. *Master Your Money.* Thomas Nelson Publishers, 1986.

Blue, Ron and Judy. *Money Matters for Parents and Kids.* Oliver Nelson, 1988.

Burkett, Larry. *Answers to Your Family's Financial Questions.* Focus on the Family Publishing, 1987.

Burkett, Larry. *The Complete Financial Guide for Young Couples.* Victor Books, 1989.

Burkett, Larry. *Debt-Free Living.* Moody Press, 1989.

Spiritual Self-Discipline:

Anders, Max E. *Thirty Days to Understanding the Bible.* Wolgemuth and Hyatt, Publishers, Inc., 1988.

Backus, William. *Finding the Freedom of Self-Control.* Bethany House Publishers, 1987.

Briscoe, Stuart. *Beyond Limits.* Here's Life Publishers, 1986.

Cho, Paul Y. *Prayer: Key to Revival.* Word Books, 1984.

Elliot, Elizabeth. *Discipline/The Glad Surrender.* Power Books, 1982.

Grubb, Norman. *Intercessor.* Christian Literature Crusade, 1980.

Hendricks, Howard G. *Say It with Love.* Victor Books, 1972.

Jenkins, Jerry. *Hedges.* Wolgemuth and Hyatt, Publishers, Inc., 1989.

Kelfer, Russell. *Self-Control.* Tyndale House Publishers, Inc., 1985.

McPhee, Arthur G. *Friendship Evangelism.* Zondervan, 1978.

Ryrie, Charles C. *Balancing the Christian Life.* Moody Press, 1969.

Wiersbe, Warren W. *Live Like a King.* Moody Press, 1976.

Suggested Reading for Part 3

Burka, Jane B., and Yuen, Lenona. *Procrastination, Why You Do It/What to Do about It.* Addison-Wesley Publishing Co., 1983.

Greenfield, Guy. *Self-Affirmation.* Baker Book House, 1988.

Leman, Kevin. *Perfectionism/Measuring Up.* Fleming H. Revell, 1988.

McDowell, Josh. *His Image/My Image.* Here's Life Publishers, Inc., 1984.

Stoop, David. *Hope for the Perfectionist.* Oliver Nelson, 1989.

van Vonderen, Jeff. *Tired of Trying to Measure Up.* Bethany House Publishers, 1989.

Youssef, Michael. *He-Ism vs. Me-Ism.* Harvest House, 1987.

ABOUT THE AUTHOR

Kathy Babbitt and her husband Dave live in Austin, Texas and have been married for twenty years. They have three daughters—Jeannette, eighteen; Kimberly, sixteen; and Dione, twelve. The Babbitts served as missionaries with Mission Aviation Fellowship in Zaire, Africa where Dave was a jungle pilot. Currently he is with Austin Jet International.

Kathy is owner of Babbitt & Associates Marketing and Public Relations. She has won numerous state and national awards for her work on political and promotional campaigns, brochures, newsletters, and speeches. Kathy is listed in "Who's Who of American Women" in addition to several other national and international biographical volumes. She has taught writing courses for adults as well as elementary through high school students. Kathy also gives seminars on life management principles and has been a featured speaker at retreats and conferences.

COLOPHON

The typeface for the text of this book is *Baskerville*. Its creator, John Baskerville (1706-1775), broke with tradition to reflect in his type the rounder, yet more sharply cut lettering of eighteenth-century stone inscriptions and copy books. The type foreshadows modern design in such novel characteristics as the increase in contrast between thick and thin strokes and the shifting of stress from the diagonal to the vertical strokes. Realizing that this new style of letter would be most effective if cleanly printed on smooth paper with genuinely black ink, he built his own presses, developed a method of hot-pressing the printed sheet to a smooth, glossy finish, and experimented with special inks. However, Baskerville did not enter into general commercial use in England until 1923.

Substantive Editing:
Michael S. Hyatt

Copy Editing:
Peggy Moon

Cover Design:
Steve Diggs & Friends
Nashville, Tennessee

Page Composition:
Thoburn Press
Box 2459, Reston, Virginia 22090

Printing and Binding:
Maple-Vail Book Manufacturing Group
York, Pennsylvania

Cover Printing:
Weber Graphics
Chicago, Illinois